EFFECTIVE PARTICIPATORY PRACTICE

MODERN APPLICATIONS OF SOCIAL WORK

An Aldine de Gruyter Series of Texts and Monographs

SERIES EDITOR

James K. Whittaker

Paul Adams and Kristine E. Nelson (eds.), **Reinventing Human Services: Community and Family Centered Practice**

Ralph E. Anderson and Irl Carter, **Human Behavior in the Social Environment: A Social Systems Approach** (Fourth Edition)

Richard P. Barth, Mark Courtney, Jill Duerr Berrick, and Vicky Albert, **From Child Abuse to Permanency Planning: Child Welfare Services Pathways and Placements**

Marie Connolly with Margaret McKenzie, **Effective Participatory Practice: Family Group Conferencing in Child Protection**

Kathleen Ell and Helen Northen, **Families and Health Care: Psychosocial Practice**

Marian Fatout, **Models for Change in Social Group Work**

Mark W. Fraser, Peter J. Pecora, and David A. Haapala, **Families in Crisis: The Impact of Intensive Family Preservation Services**

James Garbarino, **Children and Families in the Social Environment** (Second Edition)

James Garbarino, and Associates, **Special Children—Special Risks: The Maltreatment of Children with Disabilities**

James Garbarino, and Associates, **Troubled Youth, Troubled Families: Understanding Families At-Risk for Adolescent Maltreatment**

Roberta R. Greene, **Social Work with the Aged and Their Families**

Roberta R. Greene, **Human Behavior Theory: A Diversity Framework**

Roberta R. Greene and Paul H. Ephross, **Human Behavior Theory and Social Work Practice**

André Ivanoff, Betty J. Blythe, and Tony Tripodi, **Involuntary Clients in Social Work Practice: A Research-Based Approach**

Paul K. H. Kim (ed.), **Serving the Elderly: Skills for Practice**

Jill Kinney, David A. Haapala, and Charlotte Booth, **Keeping Families Together: The Homebuilders Model**

Robert M. Moroney, **Social Policy and Social Work: Critical Essays on the Welfare State**

Peter J. Pecora, Mark W. Fraser, Kristine Nelson, Jacqueline McCroskey, and William Meezan, **Evaluating Family-Based Services**

Peter J. Pecora, James K. Whittaker, Anthony N. Maluccio, Richard P. Barth, and Robert D. Plotnick, **The Child Welfare Challenge: Policy, Practice, and Research**

John R. Schuerman, Tina L. Rzepnicki, and Julia H. Littell, **Putting Families First: An Experiment in Family Preservation**

Madeline R. Stoner, **The Civil Rights of Homeless People: Law, Social Policy, and Social Work Practice**

Albert E. Trieschman, James K. Whittaker, and Larry K. Brentro, **The Other 23 Hours: Child-Care Work with Emotionally Disturbed Children in a Therapeutic Milieu**

Harry H. Vorrath and Larry K. Brentro, **Positive Peer Culture (Second Edition)**

Betsy S. Vourlekis and Roberta R. Greene (eds). **Social Work Case Management**

James K. Whittaker, and Associates, **Reaching High-Risk Families: Intensive Family Preservation in Human Services**

EFFECTIVE PARTICIPATORY PRACTICE
Family Group Conferencing in Child Protection

MARIE CONNOLLY
with
MARGARET McKENZIE

ALDINE DE GRUYTER
New York

About the Authors

Marie Connolly is a Senior Lecturer in Social Work at the University of Canterbury, Christchurch, New Zealand. Her teaching areas include individual and family practice, working with violence, and social work research. She has worked as a consultant for the Inspector General of the Illinois Department of Child and Family Services in conjunction with the University of Chicago.

Margaret McKenzie is a Lecturer in Community and Family Studies at the University of Otaga, Dunedin, New Zealand. She is completing her doctoral research in Family Group Conferences, process and participation, and has presented this work at international conferences in the United Kingdom and Asia.

Copyright © 1999 Walter de Gruyter, Inc., New York

ALDINE DE GRUYTER
A division of Walter de Gruyter, Inc.
200 Saw Mill River Road
Hawthorne, New York 10532
This publication is printed on acid free paper ⊗

Library of Congress Cataloging-in-Publication Data

Connolly, Marie.
    Effective participatory practice : family group conferencing in
child protection / by Marie Connolly with Margaret McKenzie.
        p.   cm. — (Modern applications of social work)
    Includes bibliographical references and index.
    ISBN 0-202-36107-1 (cloth : alk. paper). 36108-x (pbk.: alk. paper).
    1. Social work with children—New Zealand.   2. Family social work—
New Zealand.   3. Child welfare—New Zealand—Decision making.
4. Child abuse—New Zealand.   5. Family—New Zealand—Decision
making.   I. McKenzie, Margaret.   II. Title.   III. Series.
HV802.5.C66   1999
362.7'0993—dc21   98-46483
                                                                              CIP

Manufactured in the United States of America

10   9   8   7   6   5   4   3   2   1

Contents

Preface

In recent years something of a revolution has been taking place in the complex area of child protection work: Professionals are sharing power with families. The legacy of professional decision-making in child protection is slowly but determinably being tampered with. In some countries, for example, New Zealand, principles of family participation and involvement in decision-making have been enshrined in child welfare legislation. Here, in abuse or neglect enquiries, social workers are required not only to consult and work with the immediate family, but also to harness the strengths of the extended family in decision-making processes. The Family Group Conference is the practice innovation that brings together the family and the professional in a shared decision-making forum. In this respect, social workers in the 1990s are exploring unfamiliar territory as they attempt to operationalize a model of family empowerment within the child protection field. In other countries, the notion of partnership with family is also influencing practice in significant ways as workers explore the possibilities of increasing the safety support network for children at risk. This book is about these changes in practice.

Since 1989, when New Zealand introduced processes of family involvement into practice, we have experienced what it is like to share decision-making with families. From naive beginnings we have learned by experience that achieving true partnership with families is elusive and complex, and is a process that makes considerable demands on the energy and resources of those involved. We have also watched with interest the variety of similar developments occurring internationally as practitioners and policymakers attempt to incorporate notions of partnership and family decision-making into their work. As with most new practice initiatives, this has brought both successes and challenges. Practice experience consistently demonstrates that family empowerment and partnership is not always easily managed within certain family situations and

vii

that this is common internationally. For example, involving family in decision-making around sexual abuse investigations can be particularly fraught, as practitioners attempt to balance the needs of the child and the family with the expectations of the public. In our experience, developing innovative policy and legislating for interventive processes is only part of what is required for good practice. Practice inevitably needs to be strongly located within a sound theoretical framework. Our intention in writing this book is to provide an accessible work that offers a theoretical and practice treatment, reflecting the current issues surrounding family participation in the child abuse area. We consider there to be compelling reasons for involving family, including extended family, in the processes of decision-making for their children. We also acknowledge the dangers inherent in bringing family members together when retaliatory dynamics expose vulnerable family members to risk. Our aim with this book is to balance our enthusiasm with caution.

In order to understand the current practice ideology of empowerment and the development of family participatory practice, we begin by exploring practice developments that have influenced the New Zealand model. We examine the social construction of family decision-making and trace the history of responsibility for children's welfare. We consider this to be essential background knowledge for an appreciation of the philosophical tensions created by sharing power with families, and the social and political influences that have shaped the work undertaken with children at risk.

Since the New Zealand model of Family Group Conference has been widely recognized as a leading development in the family empowerment trend, we consider in some detail the New Zealand experience. However, the New Zealand initiative is only one of the many developments occurring worldwide. Many countries are exploring the use of alternative methods of practice that are participatory in nature, and that attempt to address the needs of minority groups and indigenous people. Therefore, we also focus on the ways in which indigenous processes have influenced child protection, and explore the variety and growth of family participatory models and practices in key countries such as the United States, Canada, the United Kingdom, and Australia.

Finally, we hope that this book will expand our thinking in terms of the future development and theoretical evolution of the Family Group Conference model. Essential to all new practice developments is the need for ongoing evaluation and critical analysis. The evolution of practice requires it. The practice of Family Group Conferencing and family participatory practice is maturing. As it does, it is supported by research and practice wisdom, and is enriched, inevitably, by the experiences of families and workers involved in the process as challenges and complexities are confronted and overcome. To this end, we have developed a model of family decision-making: Effective Participatory Practice (EPP), which critically considers the Family Group Conference process and the linking of models of empowerment, family participation, and partnerships in child protection. It provides a conceptual framework that offers multiple pathways to the achievement of participatory practice. The model is designed to provide guidelines for family decision-making and explores a new repertoire of participatory practice skills. In developing the model we hope to extend our thinking beyond the first stage of practice development, by addressing some of the challenges raised by sharing power, and working through the complexities of maintaining a child-centered focus within a family participatory model.

Marie Connolly
Margaret McKenzie

Acknowledgments

Many people have contributed to the ideas represented in this book. Certainly the work could not have been completed without the insights and experiences of the many children, families, and workers involved in the process of child protection decision-making. We have learned from their joys and sorrows.

We are also indebted to our friends and colleagues, both in New Zealand and overseas, for their support and encouragement during the writing of the book.

We would particularly like to thank the following people: Gillian Lewis for her excellent editorial work, Matthew McGurk for his tolerance in putting together the graphics, Jane Maidment for her assistance with the case studies, and Roger Maaka, chair of the Maori Studies Department at the University of Canterbury, for his advice with respect to Chapter 3. We also thank the University of Canterbury for its contribution to the funding of the project, and our respective departments within the University of Canterbury and University of Otago for their ongoing support of our work.

Note on Authorship

With respect to authorship responsibilities, Connolly and McKenzie jointly developed the original conceptualization of the book. McKenzie wrote Chapter 5, and had primary responsibility for Chapter 1, which was jointly written. The remaining chapters were written by Connolly.

Foreword

Conventional wisdom in child welfare used to reinforce parochialism. Thus, while theoretical interest occasionally strayed to child and family service innovations from distant lands (typically, Scandinavia and Israel), the effects on actual practices and service systems were minimal. Apart from a simple lack of practical imformation, service innovations originating elsewhere were thought to be inextricably linked to the sociopolitical cultures in which they arose and, absent those cultural supports, would simply not thrive in a North American context. International service innovations, if treated at all in mainstream professional discussion, were typically an interesting sidebar conversation—a footnote, as it were, to the main text. Few things have changed.

North American child welfare is now fully engaged in "global trade," with an impressive array of service innovations and evaluation methods as leading "exports": intensive family preservation services; risk assessment in child protection; concurrent planning, specifically, and permanency planning, more generally, in foster care; and outcomes-based planning (most recently) lead the list. On the "import" side, consumer preferences continue to run highest for various foreign-grown child and family benefit schemes, preventive maternal and child health initiatives, and high-quality, accessible child care arrangements. Inerest in such specific "ingredients" continues to grow, even as the prospects for identifying and implementing a unifying "recipe" for comprehensive social and health services undergirded by adequate child and family income supports continue to recede on the national policy horizon. Such is the power of compelling ideas and unwavering hope.

The revolution in information technology alone now allows direct communication between service planners, academics, and direct practitioners in ways that nurture radid dissemination of innovation. In addition, the easing of travel barriers and increased access to international literature has served as a catalyst to cross-cultural collaboration in both research and practice. Child welfare exists in a "global village" and its practitioners and students are increasingly callanged to adjust their vision to a global perspective.

No recent development in child welfare better illustrates this trend toward growing international exchange than the main locus of this exceedingly timely volume by Connolly and McKenzie. *Effective Participatory Practice* takes as its starting point a unique modal of family-centered intervention originating within and around the indigenous Maori community in New Zealand as a radical alternative to a child protection system too often deemed culturally insensitive, ineffective, and oriented in the main more to things that were going wrong in families ("deficits") than to things that were going right ("strengths"). Called by many names, "family group decision-making" or "family group conferencing" operates from the simple premise that extended family networks are the prime repositories for creative solutions to the problems of child abuse and neglect that sometimes occur within them. Through a guided process of family group conferencing well documented in the present volume, problems are acknowledged and solutions are both generated and implemented within the extended family network; typically, with the state's blessing and funding. The authors detail the sequence through which this process typically occurs, and they also explore the particular set of cultural and political factors that brought forth the innovation of family decision-making. In its original form and through its many permutations, "family group conferencing" has, in a very short time, literally swept the globe: taking root in such countries and regoins as England, Scandinavia, and, most notably, in North America. Its timing, in the United States in particular, could not have been more propitious.

Several currents came together. First, the bloom was rapidly fading off the rose of family preservation owing to a number of largely disappointing program evaluations and a series of highly publicized cases of child death and serious injury linked, often unfairly, to excessive attempts to "preserve the family" at the expense of child safety. Second, the scope and dimensions of the more broadly defined "family support" initiative offered little immediate relief to those systems struggling with their primary mandated task of investigations and dispositions in cases of suspected abuse and neglect. Third, in a societal context increasingly sensitized to multicultural issues, pressures mounted within child welfare to identify more culturally synchronous and ecologically valid methods of intervention that built on client strengths. These among other forces created an interstitial space into which family group decision-making flowed freely as it appeared to meet several needs simultaneously. It offered a method of structural assessment and intervention that:

- was family-centered and respectful of culture at its core;
- emphasized strengths and client empowerment in an overall context of permanency planning;
- was amenable to modification (in the way that some models of family preservation/family treatment were not);
- could be utilized in public sector practice with high-priority cases; and
- meshed well with other family-centered approaches with the same population, such as kinship care.

To date, multiple applications of family group decision-making have been undertaken in a wide variety of North American contexts and have occasioned a flurry of journal articles, reports, and anthologies.

While enthusiasm runs high, many questions remain:

- Will family group conferencing meet the ultimate test of empirical validation in rigorous studies with appropriate controls?
- Can treatment integrity be maintained as family group conferencing "scales up" to widespread application from a series of interesting pilot efforts?
- Have North American service planners, trainers, and child welfare practitioners sufficiently understood the specific cultural context of family group conferencing and made allowances for it in applications here? For example, do we yet understand the meaning of family group conferencing in its cultural context, and do we understand the critical components of the intervention?
- Is there a yet to be discovered "dark side" to family group conferencing that could occasion a backlash as with the family preservation initiative?

Connolly and McKenzie offer a unique perspective as native New Zealanders and as scholars of practice who understand and have been part of the adaptation of family group conferencing to North America and Europe. *Effective Participatory Practice* stands out as one of the very few substantive treatments of family group conferencing originating from New Zealand. Beyond cultural accuracy, *Effective Participatory Practice* fills a vital need by teasing out a more generic model of family practice from the specific application.

Social workers and other human service providers whose work is with low-income, multiply stressed families will find much of interest here. This brief, provocative, and clearly written volume sets the stage for thinking about adaptations of family group conferencing within a much wider context, including families with a severely emotionally disturbed

child, families with an adult member with chronic mental illness or developmental disability, and families attempting to cope in the face of chronic
or life-threatening illness. In short, there is much in this volume of theoretical import and practical application for those professionals seeking to
form partnerships with families.

James K. Whittaker
Seattle, Washington

I
The Social Construction of Family Decision-Making

1

Family Participation in Child Protection

Few would argue against the importance of involving family in the processes of child protection work, but at what level of involvement, however, is a question that creates a wide range of responses in a process fraught with contradictory pressures and competing interests. We begin this book by looking at why the notion of working in partnership with parents and families has become a dominant discourse in child welfare. The model of shared decision-making in child protection, which was developed in New Zealand and is discussed in Chapter 2, has not occurred in a vacuum. The practices of permanency planning, family preservation, and models underpinning family support services can be found in its genealogy. Here we will briefly explore this genealogy, and the various threads of family empowerment practice. In tracing this background, our intention is to provide an integrated picture of family decision-making as a practice model, and to provide a basis for exploring methods that place the family at the heart of the child protection process. The chapter will examine:

- The context for change: state care versus family care
- Empowerment practice and the family strengths perspective
- Themes influencing participatory practice with families
- Family involvement in decision-making

How little or how much involvement a family might have in the process of child protection and its decision-making can depend significantly on the values and attitudes of the worker, the bureaucracy providing the mandate for intervention, and the views and opinions of the wider society. Views and attitudes toward the abuse of children change over time.

3

Situations in which the state will intervene in family life and the extent of that intervention will inevitably change as a consequence of this. The history of child protection practice can be seen to reflect an inherent tension between over- and underintervention in family life. Finding a balance between the civil liberty demands of the parents and the protection needs of the child is difficult. Indeed, it could be argued that the shift toward family responsibility and participation in child protection decision-making is a compromise toward resolving some of the tensions (Corby, Miller, and Young 1996).

Internationally, child protection legislation has tended in the past to reflect an emphasis on the protection of the child, rather than the preservation and strengthening of the family. One of the consequences of this is that relationships between protective services and the families they serve can be ambivalent and adversarial. While the principle of helping families to remain intact is evident in the rhetoric of child welfare practice, it is less apparent at the level of direct service. In fact, child welfare agencies have consistently emphasized and utilized substitute care rather than developing their efforts toward the improvement of family functioning (Roy and Frankel 1995). Until the mid-1980s parental participation was not mentioned in the literature on child abuse (Thoburn, Lewis, and Shemmings 1995), and minimal consideration was given to the maintenance or preservation of familial links. Rescuing the child from abuse and protecting the child from the family, usually in alternative care situations, became the dominant strategy for managing children at risk. This concept of the state as "child rescuer" has been usefully explored by Fox-Harding (1996). With respect to the state's role in child protection, two opposing value positions have been postulated: "parent protagonists" and "kinship defenders." Society as parent protagonists (or child rescuers) focuses on the paternalistic responsibility of the state to ensure the safety of children and to defend them from harmful situations. Conversely, the kinship defender position emphasizes the preservation of the uniqueness of kin, and the supportive role of the state toward the conservation and strengthening of the family. These two positions highlight the fact that social work with children is not a neutral activity. Over time, child care practice will be affected by competing values about the state's responsibility to protect children and the need to protect the autonomy of the family (Boushel and Farmer 1996). This is particularly evident in work with families where children are in danger of abuse or neglect (Parton 1985).

Inevitably, the position of state as child rescuer comes with certain responsibilities. If the state assesses that a child is in need of care and protection but fails to provide adequate monitoring and supervision, then it has failed in its role as child rescuer. If the state removes a child from its family, and then the child is abused in care, again it has failed in its role. When the state fails in its role to protect children, the wide-ranging influence of the media leaves the public in no doubt about who to blame. Child abuse and child death case situations are frequently headlined by media in sensationalized ways. In response, inquiries are held and guidelines are reshaped in reaction to a climate where uncertainty and rapid change have become part of the business of child protection. Social work, and in particular child protection social work, now exists in an increasingly hostile environment. Practices are closely scrutinized and questioned. Consequently, over the past several decades, child welfare agencies have been increasingly challenged and criticized for expending massive resources while providing care of questionable quality and supervision of inadequate scope. The increase in the numbers of children coming to the notice of protective services, the spiraling costs in providing out-of-home care, and the growing realization that out-of-home care does not always provide for the needs of abused and neglected children has sharply highlighted the limitations of the state as sole child protector. The growing impetus for a more family-centered approach has emerged from these insights, as described by Nelson and Landsman:

> After 150 years of removing children from their homes in response to a wide range of family problems, the wisdom of this approach has been questioned. This questioning reflects at once a new understanding of the importance to children of family ties and a new tolerance for diverse family forms and family styles. (1992:202)

This represents a significant value and attitude transformation that invests family with responsibility that has previously been held by the state and professional child welfare practitioners. It is an attitude shift, underpinned by a range of imperatives including economic, toward a more benign and supportive stance to families with problems (ibid.:203). It is a stance where a strengths perspective (Saleebey 1997) replaces the deficit or pathology consideration, and where the permanency of the parent-child relationship is recognized and valued. Here, primacy is given to the concept of family participation as a process that works to strengthen families and achieve family preservation. This change is part of a wider development across all fields of social work to increasingly emphasize participation and to collapse distance between client and work systems. This has become known as *empowerment practice*.

EMPOWERMENT PRACTICE

"Empowerment" as a term originally appeared in the social work literature in the United States, but was quickly picked up in the United

Kingdom and other Western nations during the late 1980s and the 1990s (Parsloe 1996). It is, however, a concept that can mean different things to different people. As Gomm writes, "What can we do with a term that on the far right of politics can mean privatising public services, and on the far left can mean abolishing private services" (1993:131). Within the context of family, this question is critical. On the one hand, empowerment can represent a positive shift of power toward family. On the other, it may represent government cost-cutting measures in which family is charged with responsibility, while the state makes a strategic withdrawal (Connolly 1994). Notwithstanding the ambiguities inherent in the notion of empowerment, it has achieved a centrality in social work practice that points to its enduring influence (Gomm 1993).

Essentially, the empowerment concept suggests that some people have more power than others, and that they should be encouraged to share their power with those who have less. These ideas are not new and can be placed firmly in the tradition of radical social work and antioppressive practice. Family participation in decision-making as a practical demonstration of empowerment practice is consistently represented in the literature as a significant step forward in child protection work. It is, nevertheless, embryonic in stage, and there is a sense in which we continue to struggle with the concept of empowerment and remain unclear about the way in which it could be operationalized in practice:

> While many of the values necessary to family-based services have been identified and training has been identified that helps workers to acquire them, we have not yet figured out what empowering families means, or with any certainty how to do it. What we do know for the most part is that by seeing families' strengths as well as their problems, by taking their goals seriously, and by distilling hope for a better future, is to try not to disempower them. (Nelson and Landsman 1992:169)

Clearly, however, at the core of all enabling practice is an ability to recognize and build upon strengths: working in partnership, rather than in conflict with families. The notion of empowerment rests upon the belief that people have strengths and are capable of change:

> Promoting empowerment means believing that people are capable of making their own choices and decisions. It means not only that human beings possess the strengths and potential to resolve their own difficult life situations, but also that they increase their strength and contribution to society by doing so. The role of the social worker is to nourish, encourage, assist, enable, support, stimulate, and unleash the strengths within people. (Cowger 1997:62)

The strengths perspective in social work practice with families is central to empowerment and, in our view, to the development of effective participatory practice with families in child protection.

THE STRENGTHS PERSPECTIVE IN FAMILY PRACTICE

The strengths perspective reflects a move away from a focus on client problems toward a practice that enhances possibilities. According to Saleebey, the formula is simple: "Mobilize clients' strengths (talents, knowledge, capacities, resources) in the service of achieving their goals and visions and the clients will have a better quality of life on their terms" (1997:4). It requires a paradigm shift away from a deficiency and disease-based analysis, toward an ecological interpretation in which the environment is resourceful and the capacity for change and development is great. Of course, this is easy to write, but not always easy to do. Few in practice would have escaped feelings of hopelessness when confronted with a family who has been to every helping agency in town and whose situation has seemingly remained unaltered for years. Within the strengths perspective, these families present challenges: the discovery of potential hitherto undetected. In this sense, the client provides the framework for understanding:

> To detect strengths, . . . the social work practitioner must be genuinely interested in, and respectful of, clients' stories, narratives, and accounts—the interpretive slants they take on their own experiences. These are the most important "theories" that guide practice. (Saleebey 1997:12)

This focus on strengths is also an important theme in the development of a competence-centered perspective (Pecora, Whittaker, and Maluccio 1992). This approach rests on the mobilization of the strengths of the individual, family, and community in a focused, skills-based intervention. In this approach, children and parents are considered to be motivated toward positive change and competence, and again, the emphasis is on strengths rather than deficits. Indeed, there is a de-emphasis on pathology in that problems are considered as a consequence of wider social conditions that impact negatively on the individual and family. The family is viewed as a resource: "The emphasis on human strengths also leads to the view of parents as resource on their own behalf—as partners in the helping process—rather than simply as carriers of pathology" (Pecora et al. 1992:51).

The concept of parents as partners in decision-making has far-reaching consequences. It suggests an equality that has not been evident in the history of protective services. Inevitably, the adoption of a strengths perspective demands that consideration be given to the involvement of family in decision-making. It is difficult to imagine a philosophy that supports the parents and family as *the* guiding influence in practice, but doesn't recognize and encourage their contribution and participation in all phases of the process, including decision-making. The move toward a strengths perspective requires a paradigm shift that places the family, particularly the parents, first in the hierarchy with respect to meeting the needs of children. A number of practice initiatives support this notion, significant among which are *permanency planning* for children, *family preservation*, and *partnership work* with families. While having similarities and differences, these approaches can be seen as having a shared commitment: the strengthening and enhancing of families and an emphasis on ensuring continuity of care for children.

PERMANENCY PLANNING

The concept of permanency planning has been formalized within U.S. child welfare practice for many years (Pecora et al. 1992). Two decades ago, in response to what was considered to be the state system's inability to provide continuity of care for children, the notion of permanency planning took hold. Essentially, in alternative care, too many children were having too many placements. Multiple placements can have a devastating impact on children's development, and can establish ongoing patterns of placement breakdown (Connolly 1994). When considering the potential negative impact of foster care on children, it is also important, however, to make a distinction between ideal foster care, average foster care, and bad foster care (Schuerman, Rzepnicki, and Littell 1994). There are, and always have been, foster placements that are nurturing and enduring. In these situations, it could be argued that an alternative care placement is unlikely to be significantly worse than leaving the child in his or her own home (ibid.). However, the realities of providing and managing systems of alternative care are such that the quality of foster care options can be inconsistent and, sometimes to their cost, children can be unlucky.

Permanency planning for children in care, and for children entering care, has had a major influence on the development of services for families. It is a process supporting continuity of care for children and has been defined as:

> the systematic process of carrying out, within a brief time-limited period, a set of goal-directed activities designed to help children live in families that offer continuity of relationships with nurturing parents or caretakers and the opportunity to establish lifetime relationships. (Maluccio et al. 1986, cited in Pecora et al. 1992:44)

At least initially, it has resulted in a reduction of children coming into foster care and has increased the potential for family reunification (Pecora et al. 1992). It has, however, also had some significant practice implications. The strong emphasis on keeping children with their family of origin has sometimes meant that children have been returned home inappropriately (Schuerman et al. 1994). Further, having a hierarchy of placement options that puts family first and alternative care further down the list, indeed often as a last resort, reinforces the notion that family care is *always* the better option regardless of the respective qualities of each. Reconceptualizing the potential of foster care as an important strategy in the support and preservation of families has not received widespread support (ibid.). In this sense, in trying to increase and develop the safety net around children at risk by better harnessing the strengths of the family, we could be underutilizing, and sometimes dismantling, important services that can support the best interests of the child.

Recently, questions have been raised about the limitations of the permanency paradigm. Gilligan (1997) has suggested possibilities of adopting a resilience-based perspective, which includes the positive aspects of permanency planning, but better responds to the complexities of children's needs and care options. The resilience-based approach has much to recommend it. It provides a greater emphasis on the identification and utilization of the range of protective possibilities surrounding a child at risk and promotes the positive benefits of building resilience even when permanency cannot be achieved. Returning to permanency planning, however, notwithstanding its difficulties, it can be seen to have offered a strategy for preserving families and has provided an important philosophical framework for the further development of family-based services. At the forefront of these developments are the family preservation and family unification approaches. Within these initiatives, again attention is paid to the family as a system, to the strengthening of family bonds, the maintenance of kinship bonds, and the use of formal and informal resources in support of families (Whittaker, Kinney, Tracey, and Booth 1990). They represent further strands of family empowerment practice.

FAMILY PRESERVATION AND FAMILY REUNIFICATION

The goal of permanency for children is at the center of family preservation services. Family preservation programs have been introduced widely throughout the United States in an attempt to address not only the permanency needs of children, but also the exigency of the foster care explosion. In their comprehensive review of family preservation, Schuerman et al. (1994) have identified a number of points that characterize such programs: Services are family oriented. In this sense, the child is always seen within the context of the family and its role as primary carer. Wherever possible, services are home-based and community oriented. Hence, the development of a supportive network for the family within the community is an important aspect of the work. Services are crisis oriented, intensive, short-term, and case managed. Finally, family preservation services are underpinned by principles of empowerment. Within this empowering framework there is an emphasis on the family-strengths perspective and families are encouraged to resolve their own problems (Schuerman et al. 1994:19). Generally, family preservation programs are aimed at retaining the child within the family and providing whatever supports are necessary for the family to care for the child.

While an important aim of family preservation services is to prevent the placement of children in alternative care, they are also used to assist in the reunification of families once a child has been removed. Family reunification is inextricably linked to the philosophy and practice of family preservation and permanency planning. It has been defined as:

> the planned process of reconnecting children in out-of-home care with their families through a variety of services and supports to the children, their families, and their foster parents or other service providers. The aim is to help each child and family to achieve and maintain, at any given time, their optimal level of reconnection—from full re-entry into the family system to other forms of contact and affirmation of the child's membership in that family, such as visiting. (Maluccio, Krieger, and Pine 1991:216)

This presents a wider practice brief. The movement of children from medium- to long-term foster placements presents a different set of casework challenges. Bonds that are established during foster care need careful attention when the placement ends. Supporting the continuance of such bonds serves to develop and strengthen the child's supportive network. The significance of established bonds, for example, between the child and the wider foster family, and the way in which these are managed in the future with respect to the family of origin, requires careful consideration and mediation. The process of reunification also opens up possibilities with respect to the maintenance of kinship bonds if the permanency goal of the child is not to return to the family of origin. An important strength of family reunification strategy is the planned process that recognizes the needs of the children and families within the system. In recognizing the importance of bonding and the potentiality of enduring relationships for the child, it increases the scope for the development of partnerships within the child's network. In this sense, foster parents and extended foster families can be seen as important supports, not only for the child, but also the child's original family. This might be with respect to the provision of respite care if the child returns home, or by the active support of the child's connectedness with original family if remaining in care. Working in partnership with families is a theme that is woven through family reunification practice. While not always explicit, it is also central to the philosophy underpinning family preservation and permanency planning programs. Working in partnership has also been a strong practice development in the United Kingdom. It is a further branch of practice that places family, and particularly parents, at the heart of the child protection process.

PARTNERSHIPS IN CHILD PROTECTION

Cooperation and consultation have become organizing constructs in British child welfare practice. The introduction of the Children Act 1989 and the guidelines supporting it encourage a partnership approach that emphasizes voluntary and cooperative relationships between social service departments and the people they serve (Kaganas 1995). The legislative reform, which was described at its introduction as comprehensive and far reaching, encourages "an approach to child care based on *negotiation* with families and *involving* parents and children in *agreed* plans" (Parton, Thorpe, and Wattam 1997:34).

Clearly, this places the family firmly in the center of the child protection process. It suggests a need for ongoing consultation and introduces an expectation that family will be involved in a process of shared decision-making. Of course, consultation, cooperation, and negotiation are far easier to achieve when parties to the process are reasonable and responsible.

When they are not, then partnership with family can become a very tricky business. The concept of partnership, and within it the notion of some kind of equality, also fails to recognize the very real power differential between officers of the state and the family. Developing a meaningful partnership with family in child protection is therefore complex. As Kaganas explains:

> There are two very serious obstacles to meaningful partnership with parents. On one hand, if workers cling too faithfully to its tenets in practice, partnership might place children at risk. And, on the other hand, the discourse of partnership might be deployed as rhetoric to mask the very real coercive power that responsible authorities have over families judged to be irresponsible. (1995:9)

In the field of child protection, power is very heavily weighted toward the state and its statutory authority. The concept of partnership, therefore, is severely tested within this context. Shared decision-making, as an expression of partnership, can create considerable anxiety for workers as they attempt to strike the right interventive balance. Workers know that getting the balance wrong can have serious safety implications for the child. They also know that over- and underintervention in family life can result in them being pilloried for inadequate supervision if a child gets hurt or for heavy-handedness if a family is perceived to be unduly interfered with.

Opinions about the viability of partnership work with families in child protection varies from generally supportive (Thoburn 1995; Marsh and Crow 1998) to decidedly pessimistic (Berelowitz 1995). This strengthens the debate. Notwithstanding and perhaps because of the challenges directed toward participatory work, the developments within the child care and protection area will continue to require workers to push the boundaries of practice as they work through the implications of operationalizing empowerment:

> Finding ways of working in partnership with consumers of services is the greatest challenge that the new legislation throws out to all involved in work with children and their families. It will require professionals to consult with those who are close to the child, to take their views seriously, and to involve them in planning and decision-making. All that is welcome, for it will empower families to discharge more easily their responsibilities toward their children. (Hamill 1996:16)

The various strands of practice that embrace family participatory models within child protection, whether they involve family preservation or the securing of permanence for children, or whether they adopt the principal theme of partnership, all have within them an emphasis on the empowerment of people and families to solve their own problems. Increasingly, they explore the potential for accessing the strengths of the wider family and community as a resource for children, and as a means of developing the safety net for children at risk. Intrinsic to this is the provision of services that assist in the utilization of these strengths. Services that are sensitive to the cultural needs of communities will inevitably create a more positive response from the people using them. Cultural relevancy with respect to the provision of child protection services has become an important theme in the development of empowerment models of practice, and has raised questions about the wisdom of relying entirely on monocultural, largely Western conceptions of welfare provision.

CULTURALLY SENSITIVE PRACTICE

Providing welfare services that are culturally relevant has been an ongoing challenge for managers and policymakers. According to Hodges (1991), it is clear from the research literature that child welfare systems treat ethnic minority families differently from Caucasian families. In a review of the literature, she asserts that not only are children from ethnic minority families disproportionately represented in welfare statistics, but their experiences also differ once they become part of the system:

> For ethnic minority families, these differences include: a higher frequency and longer length of stay in out-of-home placements, fewer written service plans, fewer service goals of reunification and/or family strengthening, fewer overall services, and less contact with child welfare workers. (Hodges 1991:99)

In exploring the differential treatment of minority children and families, causal factors have been suggested including covert racism. For example, we note this comment from Billingsley and Giovannoni (1972) with reference to the United States:

> The system of child welfare services in this country is failing black children. It is our thesis that the failure is a manifest result of racism; that racism has pervaded the development of the system of services; and that racism persists in its present operation. (quoted in Hodges 1991: 99)

In addition to institutional racism, personal racism among child welfare workers has also been identified as a factor in treatment differences (Hodges 1991), and from a wider systemic perspective, writers have pointed to underpinning factors that impact on treatment of minority families, for example, the pernicious effects of poverty and its associated problems (Chestang 1978).

Western treatment services that fail to acknowledge the importance of culture are increasingly being challenged (Connolly and Wolf 1995). It has been argued that child welfare services in New Zealand have been based on the uncritical importation of Western institutional structures that are largely alien to the cultural traditions of indigenous people (Seed 1973, cited in Fulcher 1997). This uncritical importation has been particularly evident in colonized countries such as New Zealand and Canada (Scheiber 1995), but the lack of attention paid to the development of services that are responsive to the needs of ethnic minority children is an issue worldwide. In the United States, the introduction of the Indian Child Welfare Act in 1978 was an attempt to address the alienating effects of welfare practices on Native American children. This, however, has been underfunded and unevenly implemented (Pecora et al. 1992).

Increasingly there is pressure for social services to examine—through a cultural lens—different ways of helping. If services want to harness the cultural strengths of the family and the family's cultural community support system, then there is a need for the service to recognize and appreciate the cultural values, traditions, and history of that community. Inevitably, countries and their people have their own unique cultural and social influences. In New Zealand, traditional indigenous values are woven through the fabric of Maori society and attention to them is necessary if services are to find a meeting of meaning cross-culturally. Significant among these values is the strong identification with the land, the importance of kinship and extended family, the concept of shared, consensual decision-making, and an emphasis on the oral tradition. Some of these values are shared by other First Nation peoples (Connolly and Wolf 1995). Learning from and accessing these cultural strengths can help welfare agencies provide services that are sensitive to culture, and can encourage a context in which systems and communities can work together to develop the safety net for children at risk. In Chapter 3 we will look at how indigenous processes and values have influenced child protection. By embracing traditional Maori values, the family decision-making model of practice developed in New Zealand is an attempt to address the cultural gaps in service delivery and to place the family, and particularly the extended family, at the heart of the child protection process.

FAMILY DECISION-MAKING IN CHILD PROTECTION

Child protection practice in New Zealand has been strongly influenced by cultural imperatives and a recognition of the need for services to

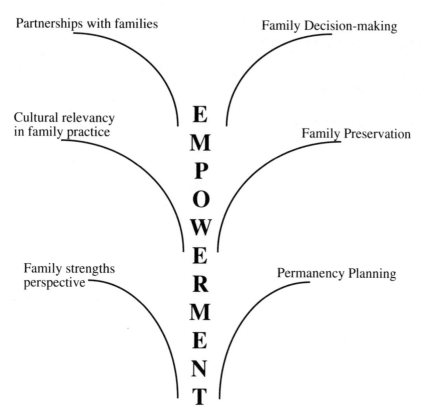

Partnerships with families

Family Decision-making

Cultural relevancy
in family practice

Family Preservation

**E
M
P
O
W
E
R
M
E
N
T**

Family strengths
perspective

Permanency Planning

Figure 1.1. Influencing themes in Family Empowerment Practice.

harness the strengths of the family, extended family, and wider community in the care and protection of children. It has also been influenced by the range of practice developments considered in this chapter that reinforce the empowerment of families and the strengthening of support networks for children. It represents a branch of practice that draws from the themes explored above, and adds a branch to the development of family practice in child protection (see Figure 1.1).

In this sense the model of family decision-making can be seen to draw from and contribute to the development of models that have a shared purpose: the participation of family in child protection, the strengthening of families and kinship networks, the connection or reconnection of children to their family and wider kinship group, and the continuity of care for children.

Although increasingly referred to as "family decision-making," the model as practiced in New Zealand is a shared decision-making process that involves the family and the state in planning for children at risk. It attempts to find a balance with respect to statutory intervention that recognizes the right of family, including extended family, to participate in decision-making around their children, and the states' responsibility to protect the child from abuse and neglect. The Family Group Conference is the innovation that brings the family and state together in a shared decision-making process. We consider in Chapter 2 how the model of family group conferencing evolved, and how it works in practice.

2

The New Zealand Experience

This chapter examines the New Zealand Family Group Conference and illustrates the way in which the theory concerning professional and family partnerships in decision-making is incorporated into child protection practice. In looking at the development of the New Zealand legislation it will consider some of the complexities of balancing state and family decision-making. The chapter will consider:

• The antecedents of Family Group Conferencing
• The practical application of family decision-making
• The challenges of family involvement in child protection

In 1989 New Zealand radically changed its child care and protection legislation. The introduction of the Children, Young Persons and their Families Act (1989) revolutionized social work practice with children and families, and established a new practice direction for the future (Connolly 1994). This practice direction changed not only the way social workers interact with family, but also the way professionals within the care and protection field perceived family and the family's contribution to finding safe solutions for children.

Prior to 1989, like many countries, New Zealand had developed care practices that relied heavily on alternative care options for children. The legislation of the time, the Children and Young Persons Act (1974), provided social workers and the police with the legal authority to intervene in family situations where children were at risk. Following such interventions it was not unusual for children to be taken into care by the state and placed in positions of alternative care, such as foster placements, family or group homes, and institutional care. The legislation and the principles upon which practice was based at that time were almost entirely child-centered. Appropriately, the needs of the child were considered to be paramount, and it was believed that the "family" was the optimum unit that could satisfy a child's needs. It was the family, and more particularly the immediate family, that was charged to provide an environment in which the child could thrive and develop. When failure was identified within the original, immediate family, the professional response was often to replace the child with a foster family unit. Frequently, the foster family would not have had any links with the original family, nor would the child have necessarily been known to them prior to placement.

While it can be said that practice was child oriented, this was generally in terms of the child's immediate and short-term needs. Longer-term needs such as the child's need for permanence, security, and identity, both cultural and familial, were given less priority. This resulted in children remaining in foster care for long periods of time, although not necessarily in the same placement. While some fostering arrangements were maintained until the child reached independence, many were unsustainable over time (Connolly 1994). This resulted in children being exposed to a pattern of placement breakdown (Prasad 1975). Inevitably, this proved to be tragically self-perpetuating as the child graduated from foster homes to group homes and then to institutions when finally assessed as "difficult to place." Alternative care opportunities have always been expensive and considerable resources were put into the alternative care system. It would be true to say that far fewer resources were expended on the child's family of origin and maintaining the child's links with its kinship system.

During the 1980s there was much dissatisfaction with the negative effects these care practices were having on a growing number of children. Children of the indigenous people of New Zealand (Maori) were frequently being placed outside their kinship network, and many Maori felt the effects of this cultural loss. A system of care was introduced, *Maatua Whangai* (literally, *the parents who feed*), that used Maori kinship structures within a fostering framework to care for Maori children. Here, a greater emphasis was placed on the nurturing of children within the kinship network, and for Maori this included the extended family and tribal affiliations.

At the same time, social workers and other helping professionals began to place greater emphasis on permanency, and on finding ways to address the security needs of the child. While this was a positive step, it mostly involved securing permanence by way of adoption, legally formalizing long-standing fostering arrangements and often breaking a child's ties altogether with the family of origin. Moreover, it dealt primarily with children already in care situations and had little impact on children entering the system. Children were still being taken into care in relatively large numbers, and fostering remained the preferred care option.

In 1986, arguably the most significant report concerning welfare issues and the needs of Maori people was introduced: *Puao-te-Ata-tu (Daybreak).* This was a report by the Ministerial Advisory Committee on a Maori Perspective for the Department of Social Welfare (1986). The report made many recommendations with respect to the particular needs of Maori children and families. Ultimately, the report influenced child protection services in New Zealand in a radical way. It emphasized the notion of retaining the child within the family network and called for family and community consultation and involvement in decision-making (Connolly 1994). Practitioners influenced by *Puao-te-Ata-tu* began to explore ways of involving family in the processes of decision-making. A case example will help illustrate this developmental aspect of practice at that time.

A school reported to a busy welfare office that a nine-year-old child, Susan, had received an injury at the hands of her stepfather. Although the child had not previously been reported to protective services, the school had been suspicious on other occasions that Susan had been subjected to abuse at home. This time the injury was serious and a fracture to the arm was diagnosed. Susan lived at home with her mother, Mrs. Simmons, who was Maori, her stepfather Mr. Simmons, who was Pakeha (New Zealander of European descent), and two younger half-siblings. During the initial assessment of the situation, Susan was placed temporarily with her maternal aunt, who lived locally.

After the social work investigation, it was considered that Susan was in need of care and protection, and it emerged that Mrs. Simmons was concerned for her daughter's safety at home. The relationship between Susan and her stepfather had been difficult for some years, and the situation had deteriorated seriously in the previous few months. Motivated by the desire to involve the family, the social worker undertaking the investigation identified members of Susan's extended family and wider kinship group. Susan's maternal family were Maori and, although distanced geographically from their tribal area, they remained strongly attached to their wider extended family, who continued to live in northern New Zealand. Living locally were Mrs. Simmons's three sisters and their families. Susan's biological father, Mr. Peters, a Pakeha, also lived locally.

The social worker arranged a family meeting and invited all members of the family to discuss the child protection concerns. A neutral venue was used for the meeting with facilities that could accommodate large family groups if necessary. Because the social worker was Pakeha, she also invited a senior cultural consultant to the meeting. The consultant, a Maori man from the same tribal area as the maternal family, worked with the social worker to ensure sensitivity to cultural protocol.

The evening meeting began with a welcome in Maori and English. Mrs. Simmons was accompanied by her three sisters and their husbands, who were all Pakeha. Susan's biological father, Mr. Peters, was also in attendance. The social worker explained the reasons for calling the meeting and also explained the process and outcome of the investigation. Family were invited to ask questions, although minimal advantage was taken of this opportunity. At the end of the social worker's summary, there was a degree of uncertainty as everyone hesitated over what to do next. At that point, the cultural consultant suggested that he and the social worker could be available to help the family sort through the problems confronting them—or that they could withdraw and allow the family some privacy to talk. One of the sisters exclaimed, "Yous can go. We don't want you fellas around here!" And so it was, the cultural consultant and the social worker left the family to deliberate on their own. It made every bit of sense that the family should have the opportunity to discuss ways of resolving matters in private. However, it was not common practice for social workers to withdraw to allow this process to occur. The cultural consultant explained that this was how things were done in Maori: the family talking collectively to resolve family issues. Time passed, and the social worker was called back by the family to answer specific questions, and was again sent away. Finally, the family called back the two workers and discussed the decisions made by the family group. These decisions included the securing of Susan's placement with her aunt and uncle, legal steps to provide additional guardianship by her aunt, and arrangements for support and access. Decisions also included the practical and emotional support of Mrs. Simmons and her sister, and the family negotiated with the social worker possible services available. A plan was documented, and the social worker agreed to provide all family members with a copy of the decisions and plans. The cultural consultant concluded the meeting with words of closure in Maori and English, and everybody finished with a cup of tea.

Although it was not realized at the time, the principle of family decision-making and the participatory process of the meeting described above closely approximated the adopted model of future practice: the Family Group Conference. Social workers around the country, dissatisfied with the monocultural approaches to child protection, which neglected to view the child within the context of the family, were starting to explore ways of developing partnerships with family and the potential for harnessing the strengths of the wider family group. Practice wisdom quickly spread. At the same time, major concerns were being expressed concerning the institutionalization of children, and care practices that isolated children from their family network were coming under increased critical scrutiny. In the midst of all this discontent, a young child died while under welfare supervision. Such scandals often seem to speed welfare reform (Connolly 1994), and this case proved to be no exception. The death was widely publicized and the subsequent report was highly critical of the professionals' lack of attention to the involvement of extended family (Pilalis, Mamea, and Opai 1988). It was considered that extended family and others within the child's network had potential to offer important protections. To neglect them was to seriously reduce the safety options available. Thus, the strands of practice change, cultural pressure, and the tragedies of protective care and supervision came together to significantly influence policy and lawmakers. The *Children, Young Persons and their Families Act* was introduced in 1989. By including "Families" in the title it proclaimed its intent: to centralize the importance of family with respect to child care and protection law. It formalized the sporadic participatory practice trend and pushed New Zealand social workers wholeheartedly into a new way of thinking and behaving. Naturally, this did not happen overnight.

At a time when the New Zealand government was in a phase of significant fiscal retrenchment, the Department of Social Welfare was allocated a large sum of money to prepare for the implementation of the new legislation. The preparation time was six months—not long, considering the paradigm shift necessary to make the new law work. Teams of regional advisors were established, and the mammoth task of training social workers, other professionals, and the community began. Particular attention was paid to explaining the vision of the legislation, its cultural relevancy, and the importance it placed on supporting the cultural strength of the family, extended family, and kinship network. It reinforced the concept of family involvement and family responsibility, and the shift in emphasis from state to family care of children. Not everybody was happy with this shift in emphasis. Some people questioned the wisdom of allowing family decision-making responsibility when, in many cases, the family had caused the problem in the first place. However, social workers committed to the new changes repeatedly responded by reinforcing the concept of partnership in decision-making, and particularly the potential value of harnessing the resources of the wider extended family group.

HOW THE ACT WORKS IN PRACTICE

Despite continued debate, New Zealand does not have mandatory reporting provisions within its child care and protection legislation. The legislation does, however, provide the means by which any person can report to the authorities children he or she considers to be at risk. It offers some definitions of what is meant by an absence of care and protection, but these are of a general nature. For example, section 14 states:

(a) The child or young person is being or is likely to be harmed (whether physically or emotionally or sexually), ill-treated, abused, or seriously deprived; or
(b) The child's or young person's development or physical or mental or emotional well-being is being, or is likely to be, impaired or neglected, and that impairment or neglect is, or is likely to be, serious and avoidable . . .

Once reported to a social worker or police, the child's situation is investigated. Such referrals typically follow standard investigative procedures. However, in addition to previous practice, the legislation introduces a formal process of consultation with members of a Care and Protection Resource Panel (CPRP). The CPRPs are advisory committees that provide advice to workers in the protective services. They are attached to statutory agencies throughout the country, and social workers and the police are required to consult with them throughout the process of a child protection enquiry (see Figure 2.1).

Appointments to the panels include people from occupations and organizations that are concerned with the care and protection of children. This includes not only people with professional expertise, but also people with cultural and community knowledge and experience. As well as providing a consultative function, the CPRPs are required to promote coordination of services to children and young persons and their families (section 429). While having no executive power, the CPRPs have the effect of providing an additional monitoring system. In addition to this, by including laypeople, they reinforce the importance of community involvement and the aim of increasing the safety network surrounding children at risk.

Returning to the child protection enquiry (Figure 2.1), following investigation, there are three possible steps:

1. the investigation reveals no concern for the child's safety and no further action is anticipated;
2. the investigation reveals that a care and protection concern exists, in which case a referral is made to a care and protection coordinator; or
3. the child is considered at risk of harm and immediate safety action is taken to secure the child's safety *and* a referral is made to a care and protection coordinator.

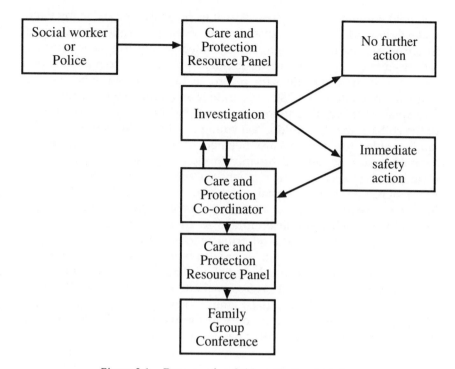

Figure 2.1. Process of a child protection inquiry.

Care and protection coordinators are senior, statutory positions created by the legislation. Their primary task has been to facilitate the provisions of the legislation and particularly to convene Family Group Conferences.

THE FAMILY GROUP CONFERENCE

The Family Group Conference (FGC) is a legal process based on traditional Maori decision-making practices (Connolly 1994). As a problem-solving forum, it provides an opportunity for the family, including the extended family, to hear the concerns and contribute to the decision-making process with respect to the child.

When a referral is made, it is the care and protection coordinator's job to make contact with people from the child's kinship system and invite them to the FGC. The emphasis is clearly on building the problem-solving potential within the family. In a sense it is the equivalent of "many hands make light work," and with this in mind considerable attempts are made to encourage family to attend. If extended family live geographically distanced from the child, assistance can be provided to help them attend. The legislation is specific with regard to those persons who have an entitlement to attend an FGC. The child is an entitled member unless the coordinator believes that attendance would be detrimental to the interests of the child or that the child is too young to attend. The parent or guardian is entitled to attend, as are members of the family or family group. "Family group" is defined broadly to include persons with whom the child has a biological or legal relationship, and persons to whom the child has a significant psychological attachment. So, if a child has been in a long-term fostering situation, then members of the foster family to whom the child is attached are also entitled to attend. Other entitled persons include the coordinator, the referring worker, an agent of the court (if appropriate), legal representatives or lay advocates, and any other person whom the family may wish to have attend. The emphasis is on maximum family attendance, minimal professional attendance. Because attendance is legally mandated, individuals, family members or otherwise, cannot place restrictions on who can come to the meeting. Only coordinators have authority to exclude entitled people. In this regard, they have sweeping powers of exclusion and can deny attendance if it is considered to be potentially detrimental to the interests of the child, or is undesirable for any other reason. However, exercising this veto is considered to be an extreme use of power and is done only after careful consideration. If persons are denied attendance, the coordinator is required to ascertain their views and to communicate these to the meeting.

Inevitably, this process of contacting family can take time and it is important that the child is maintained in a place of safety while arrangements for the FGC are being made. If the child can not stay at home, then the first option for temporary care is always family. If this is not possible and strenuous attempts to place with family have failed, then placement first within the child's known network is explored. A foster placement outside the child's network is a last resort and then the return of the child as soon as possible to a member of the family becomes a priority.

The Family Group Conference itself can be seen to have three phases— information sharing, private deliberation, and reaching agreement (see Figure 2.2). The meeting typically begins with a culturally appropriate welcome according to the particular needs and situation of the family group. After explaining the purpose of the meeting and the participatory vision of the legislation, the meeting moves into the information-sharing phase. The legislation charges the coordinator with the responsibility of ensuring that all relevant information is available to the family group.

Information Sharing	Private Deliberation	Agreement

FAMILY GROUP CONFERENCE

Figure 2.2. Phases of the Family Group Conference.

This would include information relating to the nature of the concerns for the child, the investigative process, and subsequent findings. This is often provided by the protective services worker or the person making the FGC referral. Sometimes other workers provide information, for example, teachers, medical personnel, or other professionals who have been working with the family. The information-sharing phase can be critical to the successful outcome of the FGC. Successful outcomes for children depend on the making of sound decisions. If information is held back, ill-considered decisions may result, for example, unwise placement decisions. The coordinator must, therefore, ensure that the people providing the information provide it in full. For some professionals this can present difficulties, particularly when it is seen to potentially undermine client confidentiality. Any conflictual issues such as this need to be resolved prior to the FGC. The sharing of controversial, disputed, or sensitive information may cause conflict within the meeting and the coordinator needs to be prepared to deal with this. The information-sharing phase of the meeting also provides the opportunity for the family to clarify information by asking questions, and this is also encouraged by the coordinator.

Once it is clear that the information is understood, the meeting can move on to the second phase, that of family private deliberation. The professionals withdraw, and the family consider whether the child is in need of care or protection. On the basis of this discussion, the family make decisions, and plan with respect to the child's future. The principle of private family deliberation is strongly reinforced within the legislation. Briefly, it states that professionals who are entitled to attend the FGC are not entitled to be present during the private family discussions, unless they are invited to be there by the family [section 22(2)]. It is clear that the intent of the law is that the family should be able to talk by themselves. However, sometimes families have become so used to professional input and advice that they doubt their own ability to work through problems alone, and their initial response may be to ask that a worker remain. These situations can be successfully mediated by the coordinator, who can ask the professionals to withdraw, but reassure the family of assistance if they get stuck during their private time. Practice experience suggests that private family time is an important aspect of the FGC process. There is a greater opportunity for honest exchange between family members if there are no professionals overhearing. Also, the formulation of decisions and plans during this phase provides the family with a sense of ownership of decisions and, arguably, a greater commitment to outcome.

The final phase of the FGC is the agreement stage. This is where the notion of partnership in decision-making is reinforced. The coordinator is required to seek agreement to the decisions, first within the family group itself, and second between the family group and the referring professionals. Frequently the finer details of decisions are achieved by negotiation, particularly when these have funding implications. The legislation requires the director general of Social Welfare to give effect to decisions of the FGC by providing the necessary services and resources as long as these are practical and consistent with the principles of the Act (Conlly 1994).

It is interesting to note that within the first twelve months of the legislation only a very small percentage of the FGCs failed to reach agreement. Of those, most involved dispute within the family, rather than between the family and the professionals involved. Only in very few cases did the Department of Social Welfare exercise its statutory power in disagreement (Angus 1991). When FGCs cannot reach agreement, the statutory authority is able, under the Act, to take whatever necessary action is deemed appropriate. This can include presenting the information before the Family Court.

Because the nature of child protection decision-making is complex, and because family dynamics are rarely straightforward, meetings can take a long time to work through. Often an FGC will take three hours, sometimes longer. If the process is protracted, then it is possible under the legislation to adjourn the meeting and reconvene at a later time. This, however, is done infrequently. By far, the majority manage to complete the phases of the conference on the day.

Because the FGC process is based on indigenous practices that reinforce the concepts of collective decision-making and extended family involvement, it has a sympathetic fit with many Maori families. The law, however, does not distinguish between cultural groups: all children assessed to be in need of care and protection go through the FGC process. While practice experience shows that Maori people do indeed respond well and with a degree of familiarity to the FGC process, it would also be true to say that families from other cultural groups have welcomed the opportunity to be involved in the decision-making around their children. Prior to the introduction of this legislation, extended family would not necessarily have been contacted if a child in their kinship network reached protective services. Now, not only are they advised, but they have a legal right be involved in this kind of family business. Where previously links may have been tenuous, they are now strengthened and the possibility of increasing the safety net for children is enhanced. In general, people have responded well to this across cultural groups.

THE PRACTICE OF FAMILY GROUP CONFERENCING

In an attempt to provide a sense of how conferences may work, and to identify some of the factors that can influence the success or failure of FGCs, the following four case studies will be examined.[1] Two of the conferences reached agreement, two did not, and an examination of the particular circumstances involved in each demonstrates both the strengths and the limitations of the FGC process.

Case Study One: The Jennings Family

The Jennings family had six children, aged from two to twelve years (see Figure 2.3). The family came to notice following a history of chronic neglect notifications. The school had on a number of occasions expressed considerable concern for the children, maintaining that they were poorly nourished and clothed, and that their behavior was disruptive in class and in the play area. It was alleged that some of the school-aged children were beginning to steal food from shops in the area and from other pupils at school. The children had also been found scavenging for food in the rubbish bins located around the fast-food outlets near the school. They were becoming increasingly isolated from their peers and appeared lonely and distressed in class. The family were under financial strain. Mr. Jennings worked in a factory and Mrs. Jennings, who was limited intellectually, cared for the children at home. Despite a history of contact with various social services, the children's situation did not improve. The children were on the child protection register, and many case conferences had been held, attended by the parents and professionals involved, when plans were established to address the neglect issues. However, typically the plans were not followed through and no change was evident.

The coordinator's initial investigation into the family provided information on the Jennings' large extended family, most of whom lived locally. The extended family included a maternal aunt, two paternal aunts and paternal grandparents. Both maternal grandparents were deceased. All members of the extended family agreed to attend the FGC and the aunts were accompanied by their partners. None of the extended family members had been involved with a case conference previously.

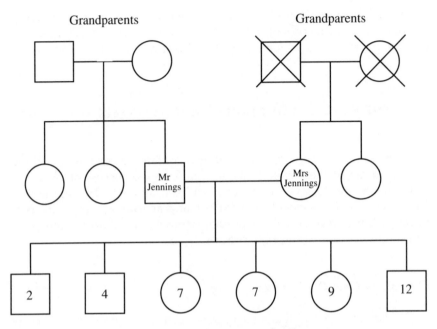

Grandparents   Grandparents

Figure 2.3. The Jennings family.

During the information-sharing phase of the meeting, the family were shocked and surprised to hear of the children's circumstances. None of the children were present at the meeting, and the worker was able to describe in detail the children's behavior at school. As the meeting moved into the private deliberation phase the coordinator reassured the family that, because of the chronic nature of the family's situation, it was important not to feel pressured into finding solutions in an afternoon. Interestingly, however, one of the uncles remarked that the situation had been allowed to go on far too long already and that some decisions would need to be made to offer immediate relief. The decisions of the conference reflected the considerable support offered by the extended family, which manifested itself in plans for greater supportive contact, child care, and financial assistance. Additional financial support was provided by the welfare agency, and ongoing supervision by a social worker was agreed to. A subsequent review of the decisions revealed significant improvement in the home situation.

Case Study Two: The Williams Family

Janice Williams, aged twelve years, came to notice following allegations that she had been sexually abused by her father. Janice is one of three children (Figure 2.4). Following the abuse disclosure, Mr. Williams admitted the abuse and moved away from the family home. He was, however, keen to return home, and Janice expressed fear and apprehension at the possibility of her father coming back. Mrs. Williams relied heavily on her husband for support both in terms of managing the home and the care of the children. Mr. Williams had been very involved in the day to day running of the home, and after he left Mrs. Williams found it extremely difficult to cope. She struggled with the most straightforward of tasks and was feeling increasingly depressed. She also missed her husband, and although supportive of Janice, she wanted things back the way they had been.

Again, the coordinator found that the Williams family were part of a reasonably large kinship network. Mrs. Williams had a brother who lived locally. Other members of the maternal family lived some distance away. Mr. Williams's two sisters lived within easy driving distance of the family. Both sets of grandparents were deceased.

All but one member of the maternal side of the family attended the FGC. Encouraged by the coordinator, the uncle who was unable to attend wrote a letter to the meeting expressing his views. Both of Mr. Williams's sisters attended the meeting. In addition to the family, there were a num-

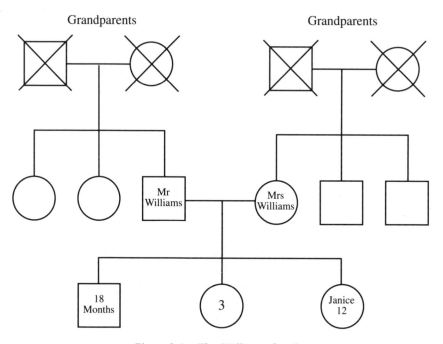

Figure 2.4. The Williams family.

ber of quasi-family members, friends who had known the family for many years and were present by family request. Because of Janice's fear and distress at the prospect of meeting her father so soon after the abuse, the coordinator exercised her statutory authority and excluded him from the meeting. As required by the legislation, Mr. Williams's views were recorded and were presented to the family group as part of the information-sharing phase of the meeting.

Prior to the FGC, members of the extended family had largely lost touch with each other, and the meeting provided the opportunity to renew lost links. Family were supportive of one another at the meeting, and the decisions reflected their desire to reestablish contact. With this in mind, regular contact visits were arranged and child care assistance was offered and subsequently provided by the family. Although the family acknowledged the fact that Mr. Williams wanted to return home, they also discussed at length the importance of Janice feeling safe. They also recognized Mrs. Williams's support needs and the conflicting nature of competing needs within the family. Finally, the family group decided that the daughter needed the security of a court restraining order with respect to Mr. Williams, and the paternal aunts undertook to provide him with support in terms of dealing with the decision. Financial assistance for the family was provided by the welfare agency together with ongoing support and supervision.

Case Study Three: The Browning Family

There were three daughters in the Browning family, ranging in age from six to fourteen years (see Figure 2.5). The family came to the notice of protective services following allegations of Mr. Browning's sexual abuse of all three daughters. Mr. and Mrs. Browning were separated at the time of the allegations, and Mrs. Browning confirmed that she had known that the abuse had taken place. Several previous allegations of sexual abuse had been made against the father, both in connection with his own daughters and a number of other children from a previous marriage. However, these had not reached the court system. Mr. and Mrs. Browning had experienced marital difficulties over a number of years, and they had developed a pattern of separation and reconciliation. Sometimes Mrs. Browning defended her husband, sometimes she gave evidence against him, and so it went on over several years. Mr. Browning had been clinically diagnosed with a psychiatric disorder. He behaved with violence toward the family and was intimidating toward protective services workers. He denied abusing his daughters, and was supported in this denial at various times by his wife.

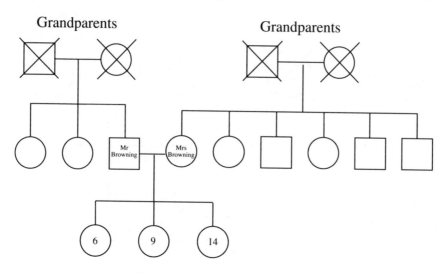

Figure 2.5. The Browning family.

Preliminary work with the family revealed that the Brownings had a large extended family. There were three maternal uncles, two maternal aunts, and two paternal aunts. Grandparents on both sides of the family were deceased. The coordinator made contact with members of the extended family and strongly encouraged them to attend the FGC. Despite strenuous attempts, however, most of the extended family members refused to attend the meeting. One uncle who was prepared to go later changed his mind following a disclosure by a family member that he had also been accused of sexually abusing children within the kinship network. Many of the family members expressed feelings of resigned hopelessness about the family, and said that the difficulties had gone on for years and that there was no potential for change. In the end, only Mr. and Mrs. Browning, the children and a family friend attended the meeting, and while two separate meetings were held to sort through the problems, neither reached agreement and the family was brought to the attention of the Family Court. Because Mr. and Mrs. Browning reconciled and Mr. Browning continued his violent behavior, the children were placed in foster care.

Case Study Four: The Gough Family

There were three children in the Gough family, aged two, four and a half, and nine years (see Figure 2.6). Mr. and Mrs. Gough were separated.

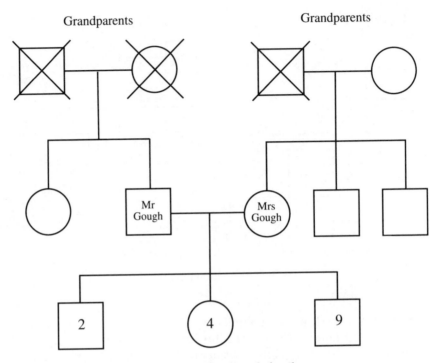

Figure 2.6. The Gough family.

Prior to the separation the relationship had been unstable and violent and the children had been exposed to severe physical abuse by the father. Since the separation, Mrs. Gough, who was limited intellectually, had been in a number of relationships. The men with whom she stayed, themselves either intellectually limited or suffering from dysfunctional mental illness, continued to perpetrate abuse on the children. There were allegations of both physical and sexual abuse against Mrs. Gough's current male friend. However, Mrs. Gough denied the abuse and seemed unable to understand the concerns of protective services workers. All three children were demonstrating significant signs of emotional and behavioral disturbance.

Both Mr. and Mrs. Gough had small extended family networks. Of the grandparent generation, only the maternal grandmother was alive, and she was estranged from her daughter. This was the result of a long-standing family feud, and there was considerable hostility directed toward Mrs. Gough, who was largely isolated from her family. The coordinator contacted one of the maternal uncles, who agreed to come to the FGC. The second maternal uncle was living overseas and could not be contacted.

The only available member of the paternal extended family, an aunt, refused to attend the conference, citing Mr. Gough's violent behavior as her reason for not becoming involved.

Consequently, only Mr. and Mrs. Gough, and Mrs. Gough's brother attended the meeting. There was considerable animosity between the parents, to the degree that they were unwilling to remain in the same room for any length of time. The level of hostility resulted in futile negotiations and even though two FGCs were held, neither could reach agreement. Again, the family were referred to the Family Court.

The case studies presented above and the practice experience of recent years suggest that there are emerging themes that influence the success or failure of FGCs. Perhaps not surprisingly, conferences that are able to harness the strengths of a wide family group seem to be the ones more likely to succeed. Clearly, extended family cooperation and interest are essential to successful outcomes, and positive FGC processes are characterized by family groups being supportive and involved in the decisions that are made. In the case of the Jennings and the Williams family, the conferences resulted in the families pulling together and providing support, resulting in a strengthening of the family network. Decisions took into account the needs of the family as a whole, as well as the needs of the children and, in general, the parents were also willing to cooperate in the planning and decision-making for the children.

The Browning and Gough family case studies demonstrated similarities that can be seen to negatively influence outcomes. In both situations there were few extended family members either willing or able to attend the meetings. The conferences therefore lacked the range of family support and breadth of problem-solving experience. In both cases, the abuse of the children was denied, and significant family members were either limited intellectually, or suffered from mental illness. Both families had a long history of welfare involvement, and the people who did attend the conferences were not positive about the process.

Giving effect to the empowering principles of New Zealand's Family Group Conference legislation has presented many challenges for workers and families. Essentially, New Zealand has enshrined participatory practice within a legal framework, and the practice has provided an important first step toward positively involving family in the processes of decision-making for children. The first eight years of practice has demonstrated that families can and do respond to the opportunity of being actively involved, and that such involvement can result in a greater commitment to outcomes. Experience has also shown that families and professionals can work in partnership and that sharing child protection responsibility can have the effect of increasing the safety net for children at risk. It is, however, still a first step, and many issues have arisen that present a challenge to the participatory vision. These will be discussed more fully in Chapter 5. The work is still evolving, and it is important that strategies be developed to address the complexities of power-sharing in child protection. Certainly the concept of family decision-making has captured the imagination of workers, not only in New Zealand, but all over the world, as welfare providers strive to make social services relevant to the people who use them. As we discussed in Chapter 1, developing culturally sensitive services has also become an important aspect of modern child protection practice. We will now consider how traditional cultural processes have been used to address the particular needs of indigenous people as practice evolves and is perceived through a cultural lens.

NOTE

1.   A less extensive discussion of the case studies originally appeared in Connolly (1994).

3

Indigenous Influences in Child Protection

Providing services that are sensitive to culture in child protection continues to present challenges with respect to the delivery of social services. Fulcher (in press) notes the overrepresentation of indigenous people and minority groups in welfare statistics worldwide and has argued the need for the development of culturally sensitive practice in the child protection area. Increasingly, addressing this disadvantaging cultural phenomenon has become an imperative and creates compelling arguments for exploring new and different ways of responding to cultural diversity. Here we will consider how indigenous processes have begun to influence practice in the child welfare area. We will look at how Maori and First Nation Canadian cultural processes have been incorporated into Western child protection thinking and how these notions have unfolded into practice. The chapter will include an exploration of:

- Cross-cultural partnerships and responsibilities
- The blending of old and new practices
- Maori influences in the New Zealand context
- First Nation influences in the Canadian context

CROSS-CULTURAL PARTNERSHIPS IN NEW ZEALAND

Originally, the islands of New Zealand were uninhabited. Scholars concur that Maori are Polynesian in origin, arriving by large canoes, some time between A.D. 400–1000. In appearance they resembled Hawaiian, Cook Island, or Tahitian people (Davidson 1983). The land had never experienced human predation, and the settlers found an abundance of wildlife to hunt and fish. Indeed, the crayfish (lobsterlike crustaceans) were *very* large by modern standards (Leach and Anderson 1979, cited in Davidson 1983) and the now extinct moa (the gigantic flightless bird) provided well for the tribes who had access to it. The settlers organized themselves by *hapu,* or descent groups, traceable by common ancestry. *Hapu* behaved as a corporate unit, together or alone, with common social and economic goals (Ballara 1998). The society was homogeneous and had a shared belief system, culture, and language (Orange 1987).

By the time the Europeans arrived in the early nineteenth century, the original settlers had been in New Zealand for over one thousand years. With the coming of the Pakeha (European settler) also came the term *Maori,* which distinguished the first people from the people coming thereafter. Prior to this point, the first settlers had no need to distinguish themselves as a group, but were identified by systems of kinship and the linking of common ancestors or events. Initially, Maori-Pakeha contact was mutually advantageous, and was characterized by trading and protective cooperation (Orange 1987). However, the perceived need for the establishment of a more formal relationship between the Maori people and the British Crown began to take hold.

In 1840 the Treaty of Waitangi was signed by representatives of the British Crown and over five hundred Maori chiefs in New Zealand (Orange 1987). The treaty established understandings between the two cultures, Maori and Pakeha, and addressed issues of sovereignty, possession of land, and citizenship. Since that time, the relationship between the two cultures has been a dominating theme in New Zealand history as attempts have been made to understand the meaning and realize the intent of the treaty. At the time of the treaty signing, Maori society had begun to enthusiastically transform itself in response to the challenges of bicultural change. Maori people were astute traders, and *hapu* controlled their own transformation and economy. However, in common with other experiences of colonization, as the institutions of the Pakeha began to dominate, the position of the indigenous people reflected one of increased deprivation and dispossession. Maori were perceived as needing to be assimilated into Pakeha culture, and for Maori this process of modernization resulted in a systematic dismantling of their traditional society. In the report *Puao te Ata tu* this process is described:

> Policies aimed at redefining land ownership, converting a communal culture to an individualistic one, fostering new forms of leadership and educating Maori children out of their essential Maoriness were rooted in the

concept of "assimilation." The underlying idea of assimilation was that Pakeha culture and ways were "modern" and "forward-looking" and therefore superior as compared with "traditional" Maori ways which were no longer "relevant." (Ministerial Advisory Committee on a Maori Perspective for the Department of Social Welfare 1986:5)

In the years following the signing of the Treaty of Waitangi, Maori land was systematically acquired by Pakeha settlers. New laws that protected Pakeha interests and disadvantaged Maori were introduced. Maori were excluded from accessing low-interest loans under the Advances to Settlers Act of 1894, which provided Pakeha settlers with the means to buy land from the government and develop it. The Old Age Pension Act of 1898 provided a pension of eighteen pounds a year, but again Maori were excluded along with people who were considered "aliens." The 1907 Suppression of Tohunga Act outlawed the spiritual and educational role of the Tohunga (priestly expert), and the Native Health Act of 1909 prevented Maori from using traditional systems for adopting children. The Native Health Act also banned breast-feeding by Maori women. At the time of the treaty signing in 1840, the Maori population was over two hundred thousand, compared with two thousand Pakeha people. By 1910, the Maori population had fallen to its lowest ebb, less than fifty thousand, whereas the Pakeha population had increased to nearly one million. It is clear that as a consequence of colonization many Maori people have become alienated from the land and that deleterious health and welfare issues have emerged. The concept of cross-cultural partnership envisioned by the treaty has not been realized, and attempts to address this are now being made in response to the many land claims that have occurred since the signing of the treaty. According to Durie (1994) there has been a significant level of consensus supporting the contemporary relevance of the Treaty of Waitangi as a founding document for New Zealand polity. He also argues:

Despite incomplete understanding of the theory and practice of biculturalism, by 1985 it had become part of the New Zealand public service ethos and had been promoted within the health system as a desirable goal. . . . The Treaty of Waitangi was seen as a unifying framework which accommodated partnership and power-sharing. (Durie 1994:101)

However, while a commitment to honoring the treaty has become almost a mantra for social service departments in New Zealand (indeed, it finds place in organizational mission statements across the country, including universities), actually operationalizing the principles of the treaty has been far more complex. Progress toward bicultural practice has been slow. Nevertheless, as discussed in Chapter 2, since the introduction of the influential report *Puao te Ata tu* (Ministerial Advisory Committee 1986), thinking around biculturalism in the social welfare area has accelerated significantly. The report highlighted the ways in which Maori people have been disadvantaged in New Zealand society, and brought attention to the insidious effects of institutional racism:

> The effects of institutional racism are graphically illustrated in our social statistics. For virtually every negative statistic in education, crime, child abuse, infant mortality, health and employment, the Maori figures are overwhelmingly dominant. In virtually every positive statistic in these areas, Maori are in minuscule proportion, if not entirely absent. (Ministerial Advisory Committee 1986:78)

The report emphasized strongly the importance of the Treaty of Waitangi as a founding document to support the realization of Maori hopes, and issued many challenges and recommendations to the Department of Social Welfare, the government organization with the mandated responsibility for child care and protection. In particular, the report emphasized the need for the reemergence of Maori management systems "with their special blendings of spiritual and pragmatic values" and "the coordination of Maori and non-Maori systems offer(ing) an opportunity for (New Zealand) to develop a unique social service delivery" (ibid.:24).

As noted in Chapter 2, ultimately, *Puao te Ata tu* influenced the delivery of services to children and families in a revolutionary way. In supporting a bicultural approach, it reinforced the need for the development of sensitive services that do not offend non-Pakeha cultural groups, and it argued that Maori people would respond by actively participating in the strengthening of their tribal networks. It can be seen that the Children, Young Persons and their Families Act (1989) has been directly influenced by these notions of participation and partnership, and has taken up the challenge of sensitizing practice cross-culturally. The legislation has tried to capture some of the traditional features of Maori society and integrate them within a modern legal framework. Although much has been said over the years about "traditional" Maori society, and debate continues with respect to what is traditional and what is not, here we base our ideas on modern constructs (late nineteenth–early twentieth century) rather than pre-European contact. There is a reason for this. Cultures develop and change, and it has been argued that Polynesians before their first contact with settlers were so different from their modern descendants that it is difficult to compare the prehistoric and modern periods (Davidson 1983). However, while some values can be found to have their roots in precontact times [for example, the importance of tribal histories, genealogies, creation stories, and migration (Salmond 1983)], many Maori values, ideas, and notions of family and family life have come from nineteenth- and twentieth-century accounts, which resonate with modern experience. Here we will talk about some of the traditions that have influenced modern social work practice and will demonstrate how the adaptations of old and new processes have been used to strengthen work with children and families cross-culturally.

INDIGENOUS PROCESSES IN MODERN
NEW ZEALAND PRACTICE

The strong emphasis on kinship and the familial ties connecting people is of fundamental importance in early Maori society. *Whanaungatanga,* or kinship, is based on ancestral and spiritual ties that bind people together. It supports and nurtures strength within the family and provides an environment in which hospitality is extended to others (Rangihau 1992). The kinship network provides a sense of belonging, a place to return to, and a place where you are looked after. In turn, you look after others. Within Maoridom, the primacy of the group is of greater significance than any individual person. The sense of responsibility toward the kinship group is greater than in Western cultures, where individualism and independence are prized, and where in general there is a greater emphasis on the nuclear family group. Social work practice in New Zealand has had to make a shift from its emphasis on individual and nuclear family work. It has been necessary to recognize children's issues as being matters of concern not only for parents, but for extended family and the wider tribal group. This has sometimes meant that Pakeha workers have needed to move from their comfort zone, not only with respect to moving from the individualized practice of the past, but also out of their own cultural orientation and into one that reinforces the primacy of the group.

This emphasis on group responsibility also has practical implications within the family. In early Maori society, large families were not unusual, and shared parenting within the wider family system was also common (Sachdev 1997). Grandparents looked after children, as did aunts and uncles. Children were not considered the sole responsibility of the parents; hence a collective responsibility for children was intrinsic to Maori family life. Because the concept of *whanaungatanga* is of fundamental significance to Maori, the fact that care practices have alienated children from their kinship system has been particularly devastating. The need to strengthen family groups and to utilize the strengths of the extended family in the care and protection of children became an imperative for social services providers. To do this, social workers began to define family consistently in the wider sense, including extended family, and beyond, into the network of tribal affiliation. As a regular practice, inquiry into genealogy (*whakapapa*), and tribal affiliation was undertaken and family strengths and supports reestablished. The involvement of extended family in child care and protection matters was also influenced by the Maori emphasis on shared, consensual decision-making. Bringing the wider family together with representatives of the state in a decision-making forum, and having private deliberation time for the family in which plans are made by them can be seen as a modern legal response to a cultural tradition.

In practice, the process of decision-making for a child is undertaken at a venue that is sympathetic to the particular family involved. With some Maori families, meetings (or *hui*, which is the term used for such meetings) are held on a *marae*. A *marae* is an ancestral meeting place in a complex of buildings, sometimes elaborately carved, where people gather to meet, celebrate, mourn, or attend to issues of the tribe. If the decision-making process is held on a *marae*, then formal cultural protocols are attended to, including a welcome and speeches in Maori. Indeed, even if the meeting is not held on the *marae*, aspects of the formal processes of *hui* are often replicated in some form, and social workers working in the child protection area are required to be knowledgeable about cultural protocol. After the meeting has reached its conclusion a *karakia*, or prayer, is said and *kai* (food) is provided. The concept of *manaakitanga*, or hospitality and goodwill, is important to Maori, and John Rangihau believes that New Zealand society has benefited from this:

> I am reminded of a book written by Eric Linklater about his travels in New Zealand, where he talks of the New Zealand morning and afternoon tea and how he dreaded functions where they served morning tea because of the large quantity of cakes and pastries. It seemed to him this was a particular New Zealand way of showing hospitality. Now I like to think that some of this has come from the Maori. I believe New Zealanders have been influenced by Maori hospitality laws. The whole basis of them is the business of showing concern for your neighbour, concern for him as a person, and therefore sharing his daily life and sharing the things of the community. And caring. (1992:183–84)

Generally, people respond to attempts at finding a meeting of meaning cross-culturally. Intransigent, monocultural practices that are disrespectful of expressions of difference will ultimately do little to engender positive responses cross-culturally. As noted in this chapter, Maori people in New Zealand have had to endure generations of cultural disrespect. However, being guided by, rather than trampling all over cultural sensitivities and protocol can be seen as a basic sign of respect. By paying attention to Maori values in the laws and policies directing child protection work, New Zealand has taken an important step toward the development of services that are sensitive to culture in the child welfare area. Operationalizing an organization's respectful response toward these values in the practices and processes of child protection has now become a critical challenge of the work. It is one that requires careful nurturing and solid commitment by managers and workers alike if it is to continue to flourish.

New Zealand is not unique in its attempts to find cross-cultural partnerships. We will now consider how Canada has responded to similar challenges.

CROSS-CULTURAL PARTNERSHIPS IN CANADA

First Nation Canadian people are diverse and come from many different tribes, all with their own unique history and cultural traditions. Prior to European contact, they were politically autonomous, controlled their own economy, and had sovereignty over their land (Fleras and Elliott 1992). Paralleling the experiences of the New Zealand Maori, initially Aboriginal-European contact was cooperative. It reflected a reciprocal trading relationship that was advantageous to both. The Europeans were vastly outnumbered and appreciated the need to curry favor with Aboriginal nations. This resulted in the issuing of a Royal Proclamation in 1763, which clearly affirmed the positive relationship between the indigenous people and the white settlers (ibid.).

In many sad ways, however, a study into the European contact experiences of First Nation Canadian people makes for grim reading. According to a British Columbian legislative review in 1992, the Europeans brought "cultural chauvinism" to North America, and notions of land ownership that masked the "most systematic theft of land in the history of human existence" (White and Jacobs 1992:14). Land confiscation effectively removed the means by which Aboriginal people could sustain and support themselves, and discriminatory laws and policies prevented them from competing in the new economic environment. In British Columbia, disease killed 98 percent of the Aboriginal population, seriously cutting into the social fabric of First Nation communities (ibid.). Colonization was clearly having a devastating effect on the Aboriginal people, as Fleras and Elliott note:

> In some cases, government policies deliberately undermined the viability of aboriginal communities in the never-ending quest to eliminate the "Indian

problem" once and for all. In others, however, this decline came about through less obtrusive yet equally powerful measures pertaining to education, bureaucracy, and missionary endeavours. The colonialist legacy has been nothing short of calamitous. (1992:16)

This undermining of the viability of Aboriginal communities can be seen acutely with respect to First Nation child welfare policy. Residential schools were established to deal with First Nation children in care during the assimilation period from 1867 to 1960 (Armitage 1995). Children who were considered to be in need of care were separated from their families and placed, for ten months of the year, in residential schools. The children were then subjected to a schooling process designed to educate them out of their Aboriginal culture. The use of the English language only was permitted within the schools and even the First Nation names of the children were suppressed (ibid.). Ultimately, however, the residential schools did little to prepare children for life in any cultural community. They were alienated from their own First Nation communities, and they did not fit into the urbanized white culture. Tragically, as Armitage puts it "the residential school best prepared children for life in other institutional communities—particularly jails and mental hospitals, into which a disproportionate number of former students seem to have disappeared" (1995:112).

The introduction of the Indian Act in 1876 and its revision in 1951 provided, and continues to provide, the legislative context within which Aboriginal and state relations exist. When originally introduced, it gave extensive powers to the Indian Affairs Department to regulate, invade, and control all aspects of Aboriginal life. Although subsequently softened by legislative reform, the Act has been strongly condemned by Aboriginal leaders and generally denounced by members of First Nation communities (ibid.).

In terms of the development of more equitable Aboriginal-government relations in Canada, it is clear that progress has been slow. There have been few gains with respect to the empowerment of indigenous people, despite what appears to be a stage of rapid change in this area. Fleras and Elliott suggest that the changes have been more symbolic than real:

In short, evidence suggests that, despite moderate improvements, a gap remains between aboriginal aspirations and political concessions. Substantial changes will not come easily. It will take more time for the Canadian public to appreciate the logic underlying aboriginal aspirations, to understand the dynamics governing aboriginal-state relations, and to become aware of aboriginal peoples' needs and concerns as "nations within." Given the structural forces working to the contrary, it may take even longer to put these principles into practice. (Fleras and Elliott 1992:53)

There is, nevertheless, a practice imperative to address the welfare needs of First Nation Canadian people and there are many who argue strongly against the brutalizing effects of monocultural practices. Longclaws (1995) talks about the relegation of First Nation people to the status of a devalued group as being part of colonization, and argues the need for a greater understanding of diversity within Aboriginal groups. He reinforces the importance of developing culturally appropriate assessment and treatment services that prevent the further brutalization of Canada's indigenous people. We will now consider some of the practices that have been developed within the Aboriginal communities that work in harmony with traditional values.

INDIGENOUS PROCESSES IN MODERN CANADIAN PRACTICE

Although Aboriginal communities are diverse, there are some values that are common across tribal nations. A holistic view of the universe is a notion that resonates across tribal boundaries, and child protection as a concern cannot, therefore, be viewed in isolation from all other aspects of Aboriginal life (White and Jacobs 1992). Children are considered the responsibility of the clan, and not possessions of the parents. Just as parenting responsibility is a shared one in traditional Maori society, in First Nation communities, specific responsibilities are assumed by members of the extended family and people within the wider kinship network. Another shared value across tribes is the consensus decision-making process, which is incorporated into each individual's moral and ethical value system (ibid.). Harnessing the strengths of the extended family in the care and protection of children has been a developing practice in some First Nation communities. In Chapter 4 we will look at some of the Canadian initiatives that have started to develop shared decision-making programs that attempt to harmonize social services with indigenous values. Here we will look particularly at how indigenous processes have unfolded into practice.

According to Longclaws (1995) the devaluing of cultural values and Aboriginal languages has prevented First Nation people from using cultural metaphors to explain and understand their world and the troubles they face. Further, he maintains that cultural ceremonies have similarly been devalued, and argues that social work paradigms need to be more responsive to the need for restoring Aboriginal values within the social services. In 1989, in response to what was considered to be deficits in the training programs for mediators within the Aboriginal communities, a working group was established to examine questions relating to mediation services for urban Aboriginal people (Huber 1994). The working group, which included leaders from five different Aboriginal nations within British Columbia, identified values that were widely held within the First Nation communities and considered that services could be improved by the development of culturally based models of mediation practice that were sympathetic to these values. The resulting model is based on the Four Directions of the Medicine Wheel. The Medicine Wheel is an ancient symbol that explores the complex nature of people within their environment. It is used for healing and self-knowledge and facilitates understanding across the human life cycle:

> It facilitates understanding of many aspects of life that can be talked about in sets of four: the four grandfathers, the four winds, the four stages of life, the four seasons, and the four parts of the whole person—the spiritual, emotional, physical, and intellectual. These sets of four are located at the four directions of the Wheel. (Huber 1994:454)

The mediation model follows the Four Directions of the Medicine Wheel, which are sacred in Aboriginal culture. They begin in the east, and move around in a circular motion to south, west, and north. The Four Directions influence the process of the mediation model, and each section of the wheel has a particular significance. The east is associated with the spiritual and setting the climate. It is where the model begins, with an opening prayer and spiritual rituals that help to harmonize the group, decrease anxiety, and diffuse strong emotions. An opening circle provides the means by which the purpose of the mediation is explained and the participants are helped to explore where they are on the Medicine Wheel. The next direction on the Medicine Wheel is the south. This is associated with the emotional aspect of a person's life within which emotional expression is encouraged. Here the telling of one's story provides an uninterrupted opportunity for a person to express or explain from their perspective, their experiences, and feelings that impact on their reality. The west explores the link between the human spirit and the Creator, and is the home of the physical. It provides the opportunity for people to focus inwardly and to understand their own needs and also the needs of others with whom they connect. The north is concerned with the intellectual aspect of one's being, and the place of wisdom where solutions are created. By exploring the dimensions, each person can begin to understand where they are on the wheel, and where other people may be. The mediation, or sharing circle, provides a symbol of wholeness, reinforcing equality and balance. In the sharing circle, participants sit in a circle and an object such as a feather, stone, or talking stick is passed around giving everyone there the opportunity to speak. The circle is sacred, and use of it requires that the rules of the circle be honored:

> While they may vary somewhat among Aboriginal cultures, the rules provide a powerful way of managing the process. The problem is symbolically located in the centre of the circle for all to work on. When talking around the circle, people speak one at a time and in turn. One may choose not to speak, in which case one's space is filled with silence. People can take the time they need to think and speak without fear of interruptions. The mediation process is not time bound. (Huber 1994:458)

By embracing traditional medicine wheel teachings within a modern practice framework, the mediation model that has developed from the working group is grounded in culture and can be adapted to cultural differences between individuals and communities.

Sharing circles, or healing circles, have also been used within other treatment services with First Nation communities. Longclaws, Rosebush, and Barkwell (1994) discuss the use of traditional processes; the Sacred Circle, the Four Medicines, and other traditional ceremonies, within the Waywayseecappo spousal abuse treatment program. By introducing traditional teachings and ceremonies, participants are encouraged to find balance and harmony in their lives, and to use the healing circles as a means by which they can identify and express feelings. The use of a sharing circle has also been used in the piloting of Family Group Conferences for young Aboriginal offenders in Winnipeg (Longclaws, Galaway, and Barkwell 1996), the results of which are discussed in Chapter 4. The conferences were used to inform predisposition reports for the young offenders, using the extended family in a decision-making forum. The conferences themselves are interesting in that they reflected strongly the cultural experiences of the families represented. A sharing circle was used to begin the process of decision-making. After the convener explained the purpose of the meeting, each person, including the young offender and the victim, spoke of the ways in which the offending behavior had affected them. The eagle feather or object was then returned to the convener or elder, who summed up the thoughts and statements of the participants. The feather was then passed to the young offender to respond to the concerns of the meeting. After this was done, the participants began the process of discussing their ideas and formulating plans and recommendations for the court. The conferences were based on traditional Ojibway cultural protocol in that a sharing circle was used with three of the six families involved in the study.

Using traditional processes in the development and delivery of services can provide steps toward a more culturally grounded practice. Inevitably, however, such practice needs to be approached with caution so that it is not a disrespectful appropriation of cultural heritage, no matter how well meaning (Huber 1994). In this chapter we have explored ways in which indigenous processes can help us to work more effectively cross-culturally. Working together across cultural differences is a challenging aspect of social work practice universally. It is about providing environments in which cultural solutions can flourish. Monocultural processes have consistently failed to provide for the needs of indigenous people, and because of this, ethnocentric child protection systems have been deprived of the potential to harness the cultural strengths of a child's wider network. A child's cultural context and the supportive networks within it can help to build resilience in children and families. Isolated children, who lack any kind of supportive network of adults they can trust, remain vulnerable to abuse. As we explore the early family experiences of troubled adults who have been abused as children, it can be seen that early exploitative experiences develop into patterns of abuse in the absence of supportive adults outside the child's immediate environment (Connolly, in progress). Building a child's supportive network includes utilizing the child's cultural support system. Cultural strengths can be worked with, rather than fought against. Fulcher (in press) writing in the area of child and youth care practice, presents some important questions that add a cultural dimension to our work in child protection. When asking "Is the child safe now?" one might also ask if this includes cultural safety. Is the child's cultural frame of reference acknowledged, and is the kinship network involved? Is the child connected to the cultural traditions of that kinship network? And with respect to service delivery, how does the service provider's cultural identity influence the meaning given to events throughout the child protection process, and how can the services avoid undermining the cultural strengths of the family so that the child is not further disadvantaged by the services that are supposed to help?

Finding a meeting of meaning cross-culturally requires a rethinking of the values that underpin our work with children and families. In many ways, what is also required is a reconceptualization of monocultural notions of thinking and doing, and exploring different paradigms that are responsive to difference and diversity. Although writing from a pastoral care perspective, Culbertson's modification of the Ten Commandments for cross-cultural ministry provides some good ideas for mainstream cross-cultural social work practice:

    1.   Thou shalt not transgress they neighbor's cultural boundaries, but treat them with respectful awe.
    2.   Thou shalt not dominate or manipulate the other.
    3.   Thou shalt not insist on your own way being right or best.

4. Thou shalt not hurry. Cross-cultural trust and insight take a long time.

5. Thou shalt listen attentively, not only with thine ears but with thine eyes.

6. Thou shalt let go of all assumptions about the other.

7. Thou shalt let go of power, including definitions about appropriate gender behaviour.

8. Thou shalt make the other more important than thee, not simply equal to thee.

9. Thou shalt use stories, rituals, and symbols, but not rules from thine own culture.

10. Thou shalt seek to offer insight and to recast roles, but not to liberate those who are not even imprisoned. (Culbertson 1997:16–17)

In many respects Culbertson is advocating for commonsense practice that is respectful of difference and recognizes diversity as a strength. Clearly when working with children at risk, and when statutory mandates direct practice, some issues, particularly those related to power and the imposition of care standards, can create tensions. Nevertheless, when examined carefully, few laws and policies are so inflexible that they cannot be worked through cross-culturally. Rather, it is the commitment to sensitizing practice that presents the greatest challenge. The use of family group conferencing in child protection can be seen as one way of sensitizing practice to culture. International adaptations of the Family Group Conference process will now be the focus of Chapter 4, as we explore how participatory practice can work across differing systems.

4

International Developments

This chapter focuses on international developments in the area of family participatory practice. Empowering families and harnessing their strengths in the resolution of child protection issues is an approach that is gathering momentum internationally. Parallels and similarities across differing systems are explored. The chapter will examine:

- Family participation in the United States
- Partnership and family decision-making in the United Kingdom
- Canadian developments and innovations
- Australian adaptations

Internationally, welfare initiatives that include family participation in child protection have become increasingly popular in recent years. In particular, the Family Group Conference model in New Zealand has generated considerable interest as welfare providers attempt to develop practices that are sympathetic to service users. It is perhaps no surprise to find more parallels than differences. Disillusionment with alternative care as a means of addressing children's care needs has been widespread as the negative aspects of foster care for children in the long term have been increasingly noted (Courtney 1994; Fanshel, Finch, and Grundy 1990). The enduring influence of family and kinship networks in the lives of children has become a compelling argument for the retention of familial links. Here we will look at how this trend toward family participation has manifested itself internationally in child care and protection practice. We will consider developments in the United States and Canada, the United Kingdom, and Australia. Although the legal systems of these countries

49

reflect their own unique development and are consequently very different, the notion of practice in partnership with family has become an increasingly important theme worldwide. In some countries, for example, the United Kingdom, the concept of partnership has become an influencing statutory principle (Kaganas 1995). Elsewhere it has manifested in the development of nonstatutory initiatives (Ban 1996; Immarigeon 1996). Individually they can be seen to be relatively small initiatives. Collectively, however, they have the potential to change the face of welfare provision as they bring a shift in emphasis from state to family care, and challenge the legacy of professional decision-making in child protection work.

FAMILY PARTICIPATION IN THE UNITED STATES

Perhaps the most significant process that parallels the New Zealand Family Group Conference innovation has been seen in Oregon. The Oregon Family Unity Meeting model was developed in 1989, the same time the legislation changed in New Zealand, and represents an important move toward the establishment of a collaborative relationship between the family and the state in the child protection area (Graber, Keys, and White 1996). The fact that the Oregon and New Zealand initiatives were developed concurrently and had resulted from similar concerns reinforces the similarities in welfare practice internationally and the parallel processes that are so much a part of the worldwide community.

The Oregon initiatives developed from a state audit of casework practice, and suggestions from practitioners formed the basis of the Family Unity Meeting model, which is based on a family strengths perspective and is underpinned by theories of empowerment. Initiated as a further option for workers to use with children and families, the model increases the range of interventive tools in the child protection area. Like the New Zealand model, it has three basic parts:

1. Listing the Concerns of the Agency and Family

Paralleling the New Zealand "information-sharing phase," Family Unity Meetings begin with the sharing of agency concerns for the child. Interestingly, it seems that the agency concerns are often shared by family members, and the meeting is encouraged to view the difficulties experienced as being concerns rather than problems, as the latter label can invite denial and defensiveness (Graber et al. 1996).

2. Seeking "Best Thinking" with Respect to Dealing with These Concerns

The emphasis in the second phase of the meeting is to encourage "best thinking" by generating family ideas that may work toward resolving the child protection concerns. Clearly, this phase is underpinned by a family strengths perspective: that the family has a valuable contribution to make and that the worker's role is to facilitate this.

3. Outlining the Final Plan for the Child

Following the development of the "best thinking" phase, the plan is outlined and documented in a way that can be monitored. It is a three-month plan that outlines the tasks designed to strengthen the family in their care of the child. An important phase in the process, it reinforces the notion of responsibility-sharing for child safety and aims to develop the safety support network of family, relatives, friends, and community.

The Family Unity Meeting model is one of four options available to child protection workers in Oregon. The four models differ in the degree of decision-making control extended to family. The models can be used independently, or in combination, based on the workers' assessment of the needs of the family (ABA Center on Children and the Law 1996). Workers have remained cautious with respect to adopting the Family Unity Meeting model. Use of the model in situations of family violence, particularly, is approached with caution given the potential for retaliatory abuse (Graber et al. 1996). However, it would appear that the model has provided a means by which adversarial practice can be moderated by a more collaborative approach as workers and family work toward successful outcomes for children.

Family Group Conference initiatives have also developed in the state of Illinois. The Illinois Family Conference program[1] is based on the premise that families can and will take responsibility for creating plans that will protect the child and strengthen the family. Pilot projects using the Family Group Conference model are being developed in Chicago and Champaign, and are supported by the Office of the Inspector General of Child and Family Services in Chicago. An important aim of the program is to protect children from state custody. It is a community mediation program in which a neutral person, a mediator, works with the family to generate plans that will secure the child's care and safety needs. The project strongly encourages extended family participation, and reinforces the notion of partnership with family, community, and state in terms of the creation of plans for children at risk.

The program is a 3-Step Family Mediation model. Step 1 provides an orientation for the family whereby a family coordinator contacts the family, both immediate and extended, for several orientation and information-gathering meetings. The purpose of the orientation phase of the process is to prepare the family for step 2: the Family Conference. The Family Conference brings together members of the family in a problem-solution-based meeting. The purpose of the meeting is twofold: to share information concerning the child protection notification, and to allow the family to meet for a confidential session with a neutral mediator. It is anticipated that it will take from one to three meetings for the family to create a plan, which is then sent to the protective services for review. The third step in the model is the follow-up phase. In step 3 the family coordinator works with the family to follow up the plan. This typically involves the establishment of support services, and a family case assistant is provided to offer ongoing support for the care plan.

While small in size, the Illinois developments contribute to a range of small initiatives being created across the United States. In Kansas, the Kellogg Foundation has funded "Kansas Families for Kids," an initiative in Topeka that has fully implemented the New Zealand Family Group Conference model (ABA Center on Children and the Law 1996). The project has been provided to explore family resources as an alternative to out-of-home placement for children. A second site in Kansas City has also been established and has been expanded to include family decision-making around difficult-to-control teenagers. Also funded by the Kellogg Foundation Families for Kids project is the Grand Rapids Foundation project (ibid.), which involves work with children of color who have been reported to protective services. Cases that have been substantiated are referred for a Family Group Conference as an alternative to court action. These and other developments point to a small but significant change in the nature of child protection work in the United States. Increasingly, models based on family decision-making practices are being utilized as another tool for child protection workers.

PARTNERSHIP AND FAMILY DECISION-MAKING IN THE UNITED KINGDOM

As discussed in Chapter 1, partnership with families has become a major theme with respect to child protection work in the United Kingdom. The Children Act 1989, which directs statutory work undertaken with children at risk, encourages negotiation with family and the participation of parents and children in the making of and agreement to plans (Parton et al. 1997). Central to the legislation is the ethos that families must be supported and that minimal state intervention be used by workers in the child protection area (Hamill 1996). This emphasis on partnership and family involvement in child protection has generated debate, with views ranging from optimistic consideration of the approach (Thoburn 1995) to skepticism (Berelowitz 1995). Notwithstanding this range of view, it is difficult to deny the developing interest in and practice commitment to family participatory practice. Indeed in many respects, the United Kingdom has taken a lead in terms of evaluative research, and has added significantly to better knowledge of the family decision-making approach.

The use of Family Group Conferences in the United Kingdom has been promoted strongly by the national Family Rights Group, and a range of local pilot projects has been developed. The Hampshire Social Services Department agreed to set up a local pilot study, which has now been evaluated (Lupton, Barnard, and Swall-Yarrington 1995). As with the New Zealand family decision-making model, the proponents of the pilot scheme reinforced the need for three basic components: that the family be considered widely and include members of the extended family, that the family be given the opportunity to deliberate in private during the conference, and that the workers only disagree with family plans if they fail to secure the child from risk of significant harm. Unlike the New Zealand model, the projects were not underpinned by legislative change, and so they relied on the commitment and cooperation of supportive workers from the protective services.

Twenty-two Family Group Conferences were held in the first year of the pilot, involving nineteen families. Lupton et al. (1995) report that the coordinators responsible for convening the conferences were generally positive about the process and saw it as a means by which professionals could work in partnership with family. They also considered that the process did much to mobilize and encourage the commitment of extended family members. Workers identified another positive aspect of the process as being the conferences' ability to shift power from the professional to the family, and suggested that the model could be used more widely both in terms of extending its usage across the country and its use with other client populations, such as work with the elderly. Mixed responses from workers were also identified in the research. Concern was expressed about the model's potential to unrealistically raise a family's expectations when no guarantees could be made with respect to resourcing. Questions were also raised regarding the appropriateness of the model for some families, particularly given the potential for it to exacerbate family tensions, and the need to ensure that plans pay attention to the long-term needs of children. Several suggestions were made by workers regarding ways in which the process could be improved. Greater training opportunities were identified, together with more publicity, wider involvement of other agencies, and additional staffing.

With regard to family satisfaction, generally the majority of family members were positive about the Family Group Conference process. They were satisfied with attendance at meetings and felt that their contribution had been valued. They also indicated satisfaction with the plans produced and felt that the process fostered family commitment to decisions. Some family members made negative comments about the confidential nature of the information shared during the conference, an issue that was also raised by workers involved. They also took issue with some of the reports, indicating that some were long or inaccessible. Some indicated that they would have preferred workers to remain throughout the conference, rather than withdrawing during the family's private time. Reasons for this included the feeling that the worker could act as referee if family discussions generated hostility. Family members also felt that they could use more guidance, and be provided with more detailed information with respect to the available resources. Significantly, family satisfaction with the process declined when researchers undertook follow-up interviews. This points to the need for supportive monitoring so that enthusiasm and commitment to plans can be maintained. Although the families expressed some reservations about their Family Group Conference experiences, the majority still maintained that they would be willing to use the approach again.

In a review and evaluation of a range of pilot projects, including the Hampshire study considered above, Marsh and Crow (1998) provide a comprehensive and carefully considered analysis of the development of Family Group Conferences in the United Kingdom. This is an important addition to the growing body of literature devoted to family decision-making and participation in child protection. Marsh and Crow conclude that the results of the experimental Family Group Conferences in the United Kingdom have been positive. After studying eighty conferences, they believe that the model can be used successfully in a range of child welfare situations:

> The families involved were no *easier* to work with, and the children no different, from others to be found on a social worker's case load. Indeed, there is some indication that the model tended to be used with more difficult cases, where workers were *stuck* or where relationships between the family and the statutory services were poor. Certainly anxieties were high amongst social workers that families would not manage to meet because of interpersonal disputes, and if they did meet there could be serious, possibly violent, consequences. These anxieties were unfounded: family members

did attend, listen, discuss and produce acceptable, often creative plans. (Marsh and Crow 1998:170–71)

Perhaps not surprisingly, they consider that the process of Family Group Conferencing will most likely work better if included within a package of family support strategies. Given the positive findings within the research, the United Kingdom is in a good position to explore the further development of the approach and it will be interesting to see how these and other partnership-based approaches impact on service delivery.

THE CANADIAN EXPERIENCE

Increasingly in recent years, child welfare in Canada has acknowledged the importance of stable, continuous and nurturing bonds between children and their primary caregivers. This has included bonds with the child's family of origin, extended family, and cultural kinship network (Swift and Longclaws 1995). The importance of kinship identity has been particularly significant for the many Aboriginal children who have been distanced from their tribal heritage by the alienating processes of welfare institutionalization. In this respect the Canadian experience has mirrored the experiences of other First Nation people similarly confronted by largely monocultural child welfare practices. In Canadian provinces a common thread weaving through child protection law has been the domination of professional decision-making when children have been found in need of care and protection. Typically, the state has assumed primary responsibility for casework planning when children have been removed from the care of their parents. It has been argued that these care practices, underpinned by legal mandates, have had the effect of disempowering the child's family of origin, and have eroded the cultural heritage of Aboriginal children (Scheiber 1995). Certainly, it would appear that Aboriginal children at risk, particularly, have been disadvantaged by a heavy reliance on alternative care as the primary method of intervention. In what has become known as the "Sixties Scoop," the number of Aboriginal children taken into care in British Columbia rose from 1 percent in 1955 to 40 percent in 1960 (White and Jacobs 1992).

In Chapter 3 we discussed the many parallels between the philosophical climates in Canada and New Zealand and the similar practice developments that have emerged. Scheiber (1995) reinforces these parallels and suggests that this has ultimately given rise to the review and revision of child welfare law in both countries. Following a comprehensive process of community consultation in British Columbia, the Family Group Conference model that originated in New Zealand has now been incorporated into British Columbian child welfare law. Appropriately, it will be used in accordance with the unique cultural experiences of the population it serves. It will, no doubt, evolve and develop and will, it is hoped, be one of many structures that will promote the process of healing, particularly within First Nation communities (Immarigeon 1996).

Although Diduck (1995) suggests that there has been little attempt to promote the principles of partnership with family after nonvoluntary agency intervention in the state of Manitoba, some initiatives have continued to demonstrate the trend toward involving family in child care decision-making. Aboriginal child protection agencies in Manitoba have considered a number of restorative justice models including the Navajo Peacemaker Court and the New Zealand Family Group Conference model (Dunlop 1996). The Navajo Peacemaker Court provides a form of mediation, based on indigenous processes of dispute resolution, which offers an opportunity for problems to be talked through with an emphasis on self-help and self-determination. Significant in terms of such developments has been the piloting of the Family Group Conference model in the area of youth justice in Winnipeg. This involved a small study in which the model was integrated into the procedures for processing young offenders (Longclaws, Galaway, and Barkwell 1996). Although not specifically in the child protection area, we discuss it here because it represents an important example of how a process can be adapted and modified to fit a unique cultural situation, and reporting their experience can increase our understanding of the model's wider usage.

As described by Longclaws et al. (1996), the pilot involved the referral of eight young people for whom recommendations of a Family Group Conference were substituted for a predisposition report usually prepared by a probation officer. The FGC plans were then presented to the court as the recommended dispositions. Although eight young people were referred to the project, only six subsequently took part, as one young person absconded from the placement, and one was considered by the prosecutor to have committed offenses too serious and numerous to be included in the study. In each case, the young person and his or her family were heavily involved in the convening of the Family Group Conference, taking responsibility for inviting extended family and deciding where and when the conference should take place. The victims of the crimes were also invited to attend the meetings; however for a variety of reasons, only two of the sixteen chose to attend. The pilot study concluded that families of young offenders were able and willing to contribute to the process of decision-making for their young people, and were able to develop reasonable plans for dealing with the offender. A disappointing aspect of the pilot was the fact that the recommendations were largely ignored by the judges, even though the project was undertaken with the cooperation of the probation services. In this sense, the project was able to demonstrate the viability of the families' willingness and ability to be involved with the process of decision-making, but was unable to find ways in which this could be integrated into the legal system.

The use of the Family Group Conference model in the child protection area has also been developed in other parts of Canada. The Family Group Decision-Making Project has implemented a trial of family group conferencing in three culturally distinct areas of the Canadian province of Newfoundland and Labrador (Pennell and Burford 1996). The pilots were well supported and were funded by the provincial Department of Social Services. Staff were appointed to run the project and, importantly, to undertake an evaluative analysis of the research. In addition, the Department of Social Services also met the costs of facilitating the conferences themselves. This meant that families were assisted financially to attend the meetings and that the costs associated with the plans formulated during the conference were also met.

On the basis of an analysis of twenty family decision-making conferences, Pennel and Burford found that families considered the meetings a success when "they were able to use the process to move from a sense of personal shame and helplessness to family pride and efficacy" (1996:218). The researchers conceptualize the meetings under the general themes *openings, standards for caring, family shame, caring confrontation, supports for caring,* and *family pride.* The first two headings—openings and standards of care—relate to the structure of the meetings and the particular involvement of professionals throughout the process. The beginning of the meetings, or openings, consistently differed from traditional casework decision-making forums. The family's ownership and agency over process was repeatedly reinforced and the meetings were characterized by welcomes and beginnings that were sympathetic to the particular cultural needs of the family. Sometimes a prayer was spoken. Sometimes a ceremony of confidentiality was enacted to reassure the family's privacy. Generally the openings were designed to put the family at ease, so that the complex task of decision-making could be most effectively undertaken.

Pennell and Burford's *standards of care* refer to the processes of information-sharing by the workers. This is where the welfare workers articulate their concerns for the child. It is interesting to note that during the meetings family members frequently felt sufficiently comfortable to challenge the workers for the lack of adequate resourcing of the family. Discussion was not merely the relaying of information from worker to family.

The last four headings—family shame, caring confrontation, supports for caring, and family pride—relate to the family's response to the process of the meeting. Following the information-sharing phase of the meeting, across the range of family situations, there was evidence of considerable shame and humiliation. This was a response not only from members of the immediate family, but also the extended family, and so there was a sense of collective *family shame*. In response to this, the extended family tended to demonstrate *caring confrontation*, which represented itself as a gentle challenging of the family members to express their feelings and reinforce their commitment to positive change. Hence, a context of trust was developed in which family members could challenge one another and were able to make realistic plans that generated a *support for caring*. This involved making plans that demonstrated considerable emotional and material support, from the extended family, the wider community, and public funds. The final theme identified in the analysis of the project was *family pride*. Having the family plans accepted by the child welfare workers generated strong feelings of pride with respect to the family itself. Because the plans were created by the family, there was a sense of satisfaction as the plans materialized and were approved. Overall, the project supported the use of the family group decision-making model for working through the complex issues of child protection. Pennell and Burford state that "by introducing the family group conference as a joint family-community-government planning strategy, responsibilities for communal care are reaffirmed in a way that attends with sensitivity to the families' cultures, histories and situations" (1996:218).

Family Group Conference initiatives have been significant across Canada. In some provinces, family participation in decision-making has been enshrined in child welfare legislation; in other places nonstatutory initiatives have been developed with varying degrees of success.

AUSTRALIAN ADAPTATIONS

For many years now, Australia, like New Zealand, has appreciated the need for social services to respond to cultural and social influences (Connolly and Wolf 1995). Traditional values, particularly the significance of kinship structures and the notion of shared, consensual decision-making, provides a framework for working with indigenous people. Perhaps not surprisingly then, the process of family group decision-making has proved to be of growing interest in Australia. Projects within both the youth justice and the care and protection areas have been developed. The use of Family Group Conferences is increasingly being seen as a valuable tool for workers trying to protect children, and according to Ban:

The rapid interest in family group conferences in Australia has occurred at the same time as changes in the child welfare legislation and the growing belief that the state can only protect children from harm if it works in partnership with family networks and community resources. (1996:141)

Within the care and protection area, Australia has consistently initiated, developed, and evaluated small projects. Particularly active in this respect has been the work of the Mission of St. James and St. John, an Anglican welfare agency in Victoria (Ban 1994, 1996). The goals of the work initiated by the Mission reflect the aims of other international developments, namely, to maintain the child within the extended family network, both with respect to children already within the care system and new care and protection referrals; and to empower families and promote a sharing of power and responsibility across professional and family boundaries. The Mission also sought to consider the relevance of using Family Group Conferences within the Australian context. Although only a small study involving nineteen conferences, the results were positive in that participant groups felt that the use of the model improved upon traditional case planning strategies: "Overall, the strong perception of participants—especially family members—was that children would be better off and that more adequate and sustainable plans would be achieved with family participation in and control over the planning processes" (Ban 1996:143).

A further study involving a larger sample is currently being undertaken, and again will be evaluated by the Mission's project teams. Findings from this larger study will provide important information about the use of the technique across urban and rural contexts. Unfortunately, because of the study's time-frame limitations, it will not be possible for it to consider the evaluation of long-term outcomes.

A particularly interesting initiative that has occurred in Australia has been the development of the model within the prison system (Ban 1996). When women are incarcerated, children under five years of age may be placed in prison with their mother. Staff of a Children in Prison program in Victoria began to question the adequacy of the assessments upon which placement decisions were made, and were searching for ways to ensure that the best interests of the children were being met. The use of the Family Group Conference model was seen to offer potential as a decision-making process, and a pilot study was begun in October 1995. The evaluation of the study is yet to be completed. However, it will include participants' feedback two weeks and one year postconference; an analysis of the children's placement; the children's contact with family and statutory agencies; and an assessment of the process of the family group conferences themselves, including the time involved (Ban 1996).

These initiatives in Australia add to the wave of interest in Family Group Conferences occurring worldwide. While the notion of family group conferencing was initially developed in New Zealand, the most comprehensive work in terms of evaluation has been undertaken elsewhere. Indeed New Zealand, as a social laboratory for Family Group Conferences, has missed important research opportunities by not establishing evaluative research projects at critical times over the past decade. Fortunately, other countries, particularly in North America and the United Kingdom, have shown considerably more foresight and have taken the lead with respect to participatory practice research.

NOTE

1. We are indebted to Denise Kane, inspector general of Child and Family Services, and the staff of the Lawndale Christian Health Center, Chicago, for the sharing of information regarding the Illinois Family Conference program.

5

Emerging Complexities of Family Decision-Making Practice

Drawing together the issues raised earlier, this chapter works through a range of difficulties that can arise when trying to facilitate family participation within child protection practice. It identifies a number of critical practice questions that impact on direct practice and the management of service delivery, and will explore the following areas:

- The challenges arising from family decision-making in practice
- The identification of critical practice questions
- The issues of family isolation, power dynamics, and cultural differences

In previous chapters we have argued that family participatory practice has become a valued intervention strategy within the field of child protection. In particular, we suggest that the New Zealand model of family decision-making practice is increasingly regarded as innovative worldwide. The Family Group Conference model is a contemporary, less oppressive method of practice, which rests on family participation as the pivotal resource in child protection decision-making. Not unexpectedly, despite the alacrity with which family participation has been used within child protection services, difficulties of practice implementation have emerged. We have characterized these emerging complexities as critical practice questions. Some of these questions arise when trying to maintain a child-centered focus within a family participatory model of practice. Others are specifically related to the management and delivery of protective services.

Given the problematic nature of the field of child protection, its concerns and history, and the frequently challenging task of translating theory into practice, it is not surprising that some critical practice questions are emerging. Our rationale for identifying and exploring these is to share experience and continue to develop the model of family decision-making. It is unrealistic to offer any model as a panacea for dealing with troubled families, and we must not deny the very real concerns of both family and professionals who engage in its practical application. The tensions and contradictions produced by a family participatory model continue to be articulated by writers in the area, such as Corby et al., who write:

> it is not . . . our view that parental involvement is inappropriate as an aim for child protection work, [but] it is a mistake to design a system for parental involvement without properly addressing the potentially conflicting interests of the different parties involved. (1996:490)

While we acknowledge the contribution of the family group conference model, we also see the need for its continued critique and development. Drawing attention to critical practice questions is a step in this process. Some of these questions were identified in the early stages of the model's implementation (Barbour 1991; Connolly 1994) and remain only partially resolved in ongoing practice. Others have emerged in recent years as experience has accumulated. Issues we consider to be important will be discussed in this chapter, including worker commitment to the philosophy of family participation; family isolation; cultural relevancy; the significance of power dynamics and how to manage them; children's rights within a family practice context; and finally, the difficult area of resourcing, which includes the challenges inherent in the financial support

COMMITMENT TO THE PHILOSOPHY OF FAMILY PARTICIPATION

It has been suggested that what is occurring in participatory practice is really a shift in the balance of power rather than power sharing as such. This movement has been conceived as "attempting to shift the balance of power in new directions by inspiring non-oppressive power relations" (Dominelli 1997:240). If such a shift in the relations of power between worker and client is to be at the core of any participatory practice, all parties need to make a genuine commitment to both the philosophical intent and the practical realities of power sharing.

The notions of power sharing and empowerment have to some extent been foreshadowed by similar concepts within the tradition of social work, such as the development of enabling relationships, and the value of client self-determination (Dominelli 1997). However, in the area of child protection practice, most protective services have a legacy of professional decision-making. Only in recent times have family been invited to those critical meetings where decisions are made around child welfare plans—decisions about state intervention, placement options, and future planning. Moving toward a shared decision-making practice requires a change of thinking and a relinquishing of power by the professional. This is not always easy, particularly given the delicate balance required when trying to meet the needs of families, protective services systems, and the wider public perception of the worker's mandated role. Facilitating the effective participation of those who have been traditionally powerless requires considerable preparation and information-sharing. Time and costs can be greater here than in previously practiced methods. Practical matters such as decisions around venue and timing can be crucial, affecting participants' perceptions of the locus of control. Arranging meetings at departmental offices during working hours can undermine power-sharing strategies. By contrast, arriving at joint decisions that ensure safe, secure, familiar and comfortable settings for the participants, and setting times that facilitate greater family attendance can prepare the ground for ongoing family participation. These considerations do not always fit with a busy practitioner's schedule. Nevertheless, worker commitment is increasingly seen as pivotal to the success of empowering practice and shared decision-making.

To administer and participate effectively in a shared decision-making process requires an acceptance of and commitment to a set of core values that may be at odds with the prior training and philosophy of the professional involved. While it is clearly not expected that all professionals should think alike, there is a need for protective services to acknowledge both the value of harnessing family strengths and the dangers of child rescue perspectives that create inappropriately conservative intervention strategies. A commitment to the core philosophy of participatory practice challenges not just our theoretical traditions but also our personal values and beliefs around family ties, identity formation, and kinship responsibilities. Enabling family responsibility, pursuing kin members to participate, and in particular privileging family and nonprofessional plans and opinions is potentially challenging to a worker's own personal position. As Ban puts it, "Consequently, it becomes very difficult for a worker who does not acknowledge any sense of connection to the notion of the wider family to be able to prepare and conduct a family group conference" (1996:150). The sense of fit with respect to a worker's commitment to these core values is therefore of central importance when selecting staff to work within family decision-making, and is significant in the provision of ongoing training.

THE NATURE OF FAMILY

Family is the key structure, the mediating core of the family decision-making process, particularly the notion of an available, supportive, involved, resourceful, and problem-solving kin network (McKenzie 1995). The absence of these qualities in the family therefore creates critical practice questions: Does the family actually exist, and, if so, is the family available?

If we examine the current statistics around family structural arrangements, we find trends worldwide that indicate, increasingly, a shift to small, separate units, many of which do not include children as constituents. The New Zealand trends in family structure reflect those found worldwide, with up to one-third of households being those of married or cohabiting couples with no children, another third being single people living on their own, and a continuing growth of divorce and of single-parent households. Interestingly, in New Zealand this latter group has more than doubled over the past two decades. These trends, which are reflected across all developed Western nations, indicate considerable dissonance between what is portrayed as the ideal family form—the "nuclear" family, considered to be a natural and universal feature of society—and the diversity of our actual living arrangements, the ways in which we structure our personal lives and family situations. Rather than the perceived ideal, our reality is often a proliferation of isolated and isolating arrangements with multiple and frequent reconstitutions.

Important for family decision-making practice is the question of how these trends impact on successful participatory practice within child protection. Clearly when we wish to involve family we must be careful to begin by asking: How does this family define itself? How does this family exist? The incorporation of family into our decision-making practices must not merely pursue a familial ideology that assumes a certain configuration exists, implying a sameness of family structure. The danger of applying assumptive models of family is that once again our professional view of what is a normal/ideal structure may dominate the individual situation. Potentially even more problematic is the assumption of a particular system of beliefs and behavior that match the family ideology, rather than sensitivity to the particular needs of the family involved.

If there is an identified family network, the question of availability arises. Do families feel bound to identify other members and to invite their participation merely because of the underlying nature of the family decision-making ideology, when their natural behavior and inclination is otherwise? And further, if this is so, does it matter? The process of family decision-making as a practice model assumes not only the existence of a kin arrangement but an actual or potential connection with members of this group. By implication, it also assumes that the client family has had exposure to their kin network, and that members of the network are available, willing, and able to take some responsibility for care needs within their family. Of course, we know that frequently the families who come to the attention of care and protection services are not generated from intact and supportive groups. This is not to dismiss them as "inadequate," "dysfunctional," "deficient," or "disinterested," but to acknowledge that they are situated in a context that is not resource rich either emotionally, materially, or practically (Cockburn 1994; McKenzie 1995). Having said that, it would be dangerous to assume that, because the immediate family is troubled, one is unlikely to find pockets of support within the wider kinship network. Practice experience has demonstrated that exploration of the extended family can lead to the discovery of people who, given the opportunity, are willing and able to contribute.

In addition to the question of family availability is the critical practice issue of family engagement, collaboration, and how a worker or workers might best access family participants. It is not simply a question of finding family and resourcing their attendance, but of ascertaining and mobilizing an *appropriate* support system within the potential kin and community network.

The emphasis on the availability of extended family and the devolution of support and care to this group, rather than the state, is a core element of the New Zealand statutory family decision-making process. Yet, as has been noted, family living arrangements do not always reflect this situation. In particular, single-parent mothers and their children are a core group of participants in child protection investigations and proceedings. It may be assumed that this represents a deficit family situation if one's view is that wider family involvement is the key to working through child care and protection issues. It is important, however, to realize that these groupings may be established by choice and may not be, in themselves, a deficit family situation. Indeed, there may be very good reason for them. Research with these women (McKenzie 1995) indicates that in many cases they are alienated from family networks, and do not view their families as sources of support and care. There may be a history of violence, neglect, and abuse, frequently leading these women to describe a rejection of family as their pathway of choice. Understandably, there may be a reluctance to ask for support and to involve kin with whom they have no wish to reconnect. Alternatively, women may describe a family that has rejected them, or kin members who do not want to be involved, who do not provide support because they feel shamed within the process of coming to the attention of care and protection services.

Both these contradictory situations indicate that the automatic inclusion of family is a less than straightforward matter. Each situation needs to be considered carefully, and protection for vulnerable family members provided. A high level of skill and commitment to the process is necessary from workers involved, walking a fine line between best practice and ideology, and between the provision of requisite child protection and potential family reunification.

POWER DYNAMICS

The incorporation of participatory concepts into our practice does not remove the need to be mindful of the potential existence of unequal power relations. Legislating for equality or providing guidelines for family involvement is insufficient to ensure participatory practice. Power issues are likely to exist within family systems, within worker systems, and between family and worker systems. For example, as child protection social workers are still required to perform statutory functions, the authority and social control inherent in such a role inevitably contradicts power-sharing practices. This can lead to conflict. Equality can be hard to enforce in stressful, conflictual situations such as abuse allegations and protection situations. The voices of the less powerful, often the women, almost always the children, may not be heard. The absence of open conflict or dissenting opinion may be construed as consensus rather than as difficulties in challenging the opinion of the more powerful, whether professionals or dominant family members. Research findings in both the United Kingdom and New Zealand (Corby et al. 1996; McKenzie 1995) are suggesting that the participatory conference and the opportunity of partnership in a joint decision-making process can of itself have a powerful effect in silencing dissent and alternative views, both between family members and between family members and professionals. Thus it is essential to adopt an approach that explicitly acknowledges any existing or potential power differentials and/or dissent in each individual situation. Explicit acknowledgment of such issues can then be constructed as a positive part of the process toward satisfactory resolution. Such approaches are seen as "working in anti-oppressive ways requir[ing] sensitivity, awareness of and a commitment to ending relations of domination and subordination" (Dominelli 1997:247).

There is a delicate balance to be achieved between state and family power in the making of binding decisions in child protection matters. There is little doubt that the process of family decision-making does much to remove the discretionary, paternalistic power of professionals. It also has the effect of increasing direct professional accountability to the family. Nevertheless, it is suggested by many practitioners that family members still turn to the professionals to provide recommendations in child care and protection decision-making. This is often over and above the requirement for professionals to participate in the information-sharing phase of the process (Robertson 1996; Corby et al. 1996; McKenzie 1995). A high level of worker skill is thus required in negotiating such potential tensions between professional statutory obligation and family autonomy, rights, and responsibilities. This remains a crucial dilemma in child protection work within a family empowerment context.

Notions of empowerment and devolution of decision-making can rest uneasily with the reality of statutory authority and responsibility. Curiously, the process of decision-making adopted in the New Zealand model can be seen to demonstrate both considerations. Working through the steps of the formal Family Group Conference can be seen as a process of negotiation where conflicts can be raised and resolved in a structured and systematic manner, thus enhancing the potential for true empowerment (Corby et al. 1996:490). It has been argued that the New Zealand law, in retaining the professional right to disagree to plans developed in the Family Group Conference, is a continuation of the negative, gate-keeping, professional imposition, which countermands the process of empowering practice (Hassall 1996). However, it can also be seen as an attempt to manage the delicate balance between professional and family power in decision-making where both professional *and* family have the mandate to agree or disagree with decisions and plans.

CULTURAL RELEVANCY

Central to the uniqueness of the New Zealand model of family participation or partnership is the Family Group Conference, a structure derived from traditional indigenous (Maori) notions of decision-making. Since the New Zealand model of family group conferencing has been developed within a particular cultural milieu, the question arises as to whether this process is appropriate or desirable cross-culturally. While this is clearly an important question in terms of the model's international applicability, it is also a question that practice in New Zealand has had to address. For example, is this model based on a historical indigenous process that is no longer relevant to modern family life, either European or Maori?

We need to consider whether processes such as the Family Group Conference are based upon a "native" frame of family process that may not be valid in today's world or, indeed, whether the model has been changed so much to fit the institution that it is no longer relevant to either indigenous or other groups. The changing nature of culture has to be considered. New Zealand's family decision-making process is based on a traditional indigenous model of extended family. The existence, availability of, and connection with an extended kin network is assumed. Can this assumption be justified for an indigenous culture, the members of which have been subject to decades of assimilative practice that has eroded core cultural values and practices?

The critical practice question then, is one of imposition of traditional values in a postmodern world. Can we realistically assume that Maori (or any indigenous group) will operate in traditional, indigenous decision-making processes? Current Maori writers are engaging with this debate, suggesting that it is threatening and discriminatory to prescribe these ways of working to Maori who are moving forward rather than caught in revival of traditional values (Matahaere 1995; Bradley 1994, 1995). This reminds us that in New Zealand today not all Maori are *whanau* (extended family) or *iwi* (tribe) based; rather there is a wide variety of experience and access to such structures.

Closely related is the question whether there is a system that fits all cultures. In New Zealand it is clear that the process of family decision-making provides a sympathetic fit with many Maori families. Practice experience, however, indicates that despite the relative alienation and individualist nature of some family groups (for example, families of European origin where values of self-determination may supersede extended family responsibility), people are responding to the participatory opportunities of the process. We must acknowledge, however, that no model can hope to fit and accommodate the needs of all families. The challenge is to find a process of best practice that is sensitive to difference and is sufficiently flexible to adapt to diverse needs and demands.

CHILDREN'S PARTICIPATION AND RIGHTS

Using partnership concepts within child protection requires the practitioner to explore the boundaries of participatory practice. This includes paying attention to the rights and needs of the child. How do we help facilitate a process of empowerment for children when, as Kroll states, "[C]hildren are among the most oppressed members of society, overpowered—often literally and frequently metaphorically—by parents and by other grownups in their orbit" (1995:90). An earlier practice question examined the issues of power imbalance and involving vulnerable members actively in the participatory process. Children are a specific group where vulnerability is of great concern. Family decision-making processes provide for a much expanded role for children, actively moving toward reducing the invisibility and voicelessness of children in care and protection proceedings.

Past practices, characterized as "paternalistic, protective and primarily adult-defined" (Taylor 1997:15) were based on the traditional view that children were of limited capability. It is argued that this perspective must now be adjusted to accommodate the child's point of view (Taylor 1997). However, managing participatory practice with children can test the boundaries of child and family culture. Families have different cultures and views about children, and the question of whose culture has precedence within the child protection milieu can create practice dilemmas. Operational rules around the role and place of children, and the ability of children to give an opinion, may well differ from family to family. They may also differ cross-culturally. The family decision-making process enables children's opinions to be heard, even demands this where possible. Yet within some traditional indigenous practices, for example, some Pacific Island cultures, children's opinions are not privileged, and disagreement with adults and elders is not necessarily sanctioned.

How then, do we ensure that we hear the voice of the child within the family context? Of equal importance, how do we protect the child should she or he voice opinions that run counter to those of the stronger, adult members of a family group conference? Current practice still has much to do in terms of giving effect to the participatory role of children within the child protection process. Central to this is the notion of the paramountcy of the child's best interests, and the conflict between protecting the interests of the abused or neglected child, and strengthening and supporting the family so that they will be able to provide the necessarily care and protection for the child.

The complexity of this practice dilemma is highlighted when considering the recent emphasis eminent writers within the field of childhood sociology have put on incorporating children's perspectives in decision-making. For example, Garbarino, Stott, et al. (1992:8) write, "[C]hildren can tell us more than we thought possible if we adults are willing and able to play our part." This acknowledges the key role that competent and empathic adults have in maximizing the degree to which children can participate in the legal processes (Taylor 1997:15). The key task in child protection family decision-making situations becomes the facilitation of empowerment yet maintenance of a child-centered focus, without undue protectiveness. Thus with regard to the child's presence and involvement in the process, discretionary power to exclude the child must only be exercised with great caution. The rights and interests of all family members must be considered, and there is a potential for collusion in silencing the child's voice.

RESOURCING ISSUES

Inevitably, the adequacy of resourcing is a critical issue with respect to the viability of family decision-making processes. This is true of course for child care and protection services more generally. Initially in New Zealand there was a strong commitment by the government to resourcing the Family Group Conference process. Indeed, considerable financial resources were devoted to the implementation of the legislation at a time of significant retrenchment in the public sector. However, this initial high level of support has not been maintained, and workers have faced severe reductions in their available budgets for both setting up conferences and resourcing decisions. The process of family group conferencing can be expensive in terms of personnel and time and with regard to the funding of attendance of family and staff at meetings. New Zealand has a highly mobile population and getting people to and from conferences sometimes requires expensive air travel. Due to budgetary constraints, there is a danger that decisions about family attendance might be made on financial grounds rather than on the core values of participatory practice. A lack of resourcing could result in family members being invited because they are considered to be potential placement options. This not only preempts decision-making, but also neglects a rich problem-solving resource in the form of extended family involvement.

A further resourcing issue is the need for a range of supportive services and programs to enable families to succeed with their newfound responsibilities. Families who move through the care and protection system tend to be those who do not have a wide resource base from which to manage. Thus short-term relief services and long-term supportive and educational programs continue to be indicated as an umbrella to successful family empowerment. The notion of partnership suggests a role for state provision that includes the continued development of necessary services. However, in New Zealand and other countries, rather than there being a development of services to support family care and responsibility, there has been a dismantling of the umbrella of support. Further, the development of family participatory models of practice has been accompanied by a corresponding philosophical shift from state to family and community care. Critics link this to the overall rollback of state intervention occurring around the world and evidenced by cuts in welfare spending that are currently economically fashionable in many countries (Morris, Maxwell, Hudson, and Galaway 1996; Cheyne, O'Brien, and Belgrave 1997). Thus a policy and practice that shifts the burden of funding from state to families and the community can seem very appealing to a government that wishes to prune its spending. A variety of resourcing practices seems to have developed, with different countries placing differing emphasis on the resourcing both of decision-making conferences and follow-up intervention plans that arise out of the conferences.

Resourcing issues always seem to interfere with best practice developments. With respect to participatory practice with families, a critical question remains: Can the philosophical shift toward economic rationalism and individualism, intersecting with empowerment philosophy—and all of these philosophies have wide appeal at the theoretical level—be translated into adequate provision of child protection systems? As with most methods of practice, empowerment models move along a continuum of resourcing demands. These extend from minimally expensive empowerment practices, for example, involving family members in decision-making processes and exploring antioppressive methods of intervention, to the more expensive funding of decisions and plans. Workers wishing to embrace empowering practices can find ways to incorporate these notions into day-to-day work with families. However, any practice innovations that involve changes to structure, coordinating of practices, and intensive support work will inevitably depend on a level of philosophical commitment that is underpinned by adequate resourcing.

In conclusion, the raising of critical practice questions such as those discussed above should be understood as a measure of the maturity of a system, not of its failure. In many ways, New Zealand has been stylized as a "social laboratory" in which the practice of family decision-making can be explored in a consistent and comprehensive way. This has also resulted from a disposition toward being first and reflecting later. Rather than proceeding cautiously by developing small-scale pilot projects, the New Zealand approach has been to enact a fully statutory participation process early in the development of contemporary child protection legislation and practice. We consider that this poses both advantages and disadvantages. By implementing a radical approach, we have learned much and quickly, and have led the way in establishing participatory processes. These practices have been demanded by recent theoretical developments in social work, by cultural imperatives made more forceful due to New Zealand's commitment to the Treaty of Waitangi, and also by the increasing push from the wide range of participant consumer rights groups. Our ground-breaking experience means we are now in a position to pause, reflect, and engage in the process of fine-tuning. The danger would be to assume that we got everything correct the first time, thus denying the possibility for growth or change. Truly effective social policy, and legislation that puts it into practice, needs to be responsive to ongoing needs and reflexive feedback. We now have the opportunity to deliberate, critically reflect, consult users of the policy, and incorporate these responses into developing the model. This is a further step within the process of emancipatory practice that moves us beyond the exploration of a good idea, to working through the complexities of participatory practice.

II

Effective Participatory Practice

6
Visionary Professional Practice

Taking into consideration the critical practice questions discussed in Chapter 5, this chapter introduces a model of practice, Effective Participatory Practice, that builds on the process of family decision-making. Here we identify what we consider to be the central requirements of professional practice in the achievement of positive outcomes for children and families, and provide a conceptual framework within which a new repertoire of participatory practice skills can be developed. The central requirements of practice to be explored are:

- Identifying skills and generating hope
- Blending professional and family skills and establishing partnerships
- Managing issues of power in family systems and family/worker systems
- Protecting vulnerable family members
- Empowering and encouraging participatory practice

INFLUENCING THEORETICAL FRAMEWORKS

The Effective Participatory Practice (EPP) model has been developed from the family decision-making approach to work with families, described in Chapter 2. It acknowledges the complexities of seeking family-based solutions while maintaining a child safety focus. Our aim in developing the model is to address these complexities within its conceptual framework, and to incorporate them into a new repertoire of participatory practice skills, based on notions of partnership.

From a wider theoretical perspective, EPP is influenced by the ecological approach to family practice (Germain 1991; Pecora et al. 1992). In its most general terms this approach focuses on the interactive processes that connect the individual to the wider environment. Carel Germain (1991) is one of the major proponents of the ecological approach with regard to social work. Her theory of human development within the social environment provides a tractable model that adds to our understanding of the processes of transition and change within family systems. It also offers a sympathetic fit with modern social work values. The theory reinforces the important interplay of factors that contribute to development (see Figure 6.1).

Within this perspective, biological processes are inextricably linked to, and better understood by their relationship with, the cultural and social context of the family, the constraints and opportunities provided by the environment, and the influencing historical context. These ideas have developed further from Germain and Gitterman's earlier work (1980), which formulated a "life model" of practice within an ecological systems theory perspective. The ecological perspective has in addition been influential in understanding the multivariate explanations for the etiology of child maltreatment: "[E]cological models regard child maltreatment not as the result of a single factor or system but as the consequence of interactions between multiple factors and systems" (Gil 1996:xii). As such, the ecological perspective provides a framework for understanding the interactive processes within families, and offers a wider analysis of maltreatment causality.

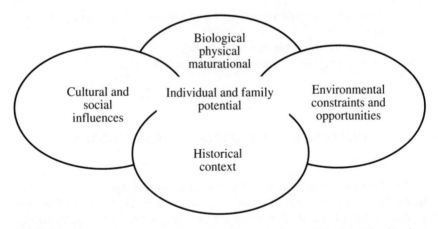

Figure 6.1.   The complex interplay of factors in individual and family development.

Systems theory has also influenced EPP. This theory provides a framework for understanding the nature of interactive processes both within human dynamics and in terms of their interface with the outside world: "Systems theories offer a context for . . . showing how public and private interact, how various change agents might be involved, and that workers and their agencies might themselves be targets for change" (Payne 1997:141). While not offering a method of intervention, systems theory provides an integrated conceptual framework that helps to describe processes of stasis and change, and it suggests how interventive change can be effected.

Transgenerational systems theory, with its emphasis on the strengthening of familial resources for nurturance and competence over time (Lieberman 1979), has also influenced the EPP model. Here, change is conceptualized broadly, and the focus on competence includes the enhancement of family self-confidence and self-esteem, the successful negotiation of life-course tasks, and attention to the provision of parental and family guidance to children and young people.

Finally, EPP is strongly influenced by empowerment models of practice and antioppressive approaches to social work. Empowerment principles are central to the family participatory model. According to Payne,

[empowerment] seeks to help clients gain power of decision and action over their own lives by reducing the effect of social or personal blocks to exercising existing power, by increasing capacity and self-confidence to use power and by transferring power from the environment to clients. (1997:266)

Empowerment models of practice have been of growing significance to social work in recent years. As discussed in Chapter 1, the term *empowerment* has only recently been seen in practice literature, gaining prominence in the 1990s. According to Adams,

empowerment in all domains and sectors of practice could be, if it has not already become, *the* central, energising feature of social work. It is central to social work theory and practice. It has a legitimate place in all aspects of social work. In many situations, without empowerment, it could be argued that something fundamental is missing from the social work being practiced. (1996:2–3)

THE PARTICIPATORY APPROACH

Within the child protection area, the issue of family empowerment is crucial, but inevitably complex. Family empowerment has to do with families having agency over decisions affecting their lives. It means families sharing power and professionals conceding power. Managing family dynamics is frequently difficult, but particularly so in the decision-making area of child protection. Developing Effective Participatory Practice with families makes many demands of the professionals as it places them directly within the family system.

Participatory practice skills are based on notions of partnership, and as such require the worker to view the family as a valuable unit that can positively contribute to the process of decision-making. A focus on the family's strengths, rather than deficits, is an important shift in emphasis, wherein the family becomes a resource that has the potential to increase the safety net for children at risk. Professionals alone, because they are unable to provide adequate oversight, cannot realistically protect children. Indeed, professional strategies for surveillance are often woefully inadequate, sometimes amounting to a weekly visit. In the face of these realities, building a safety net that includes a range of resources becomes an imperative. Family, in both the immediate and wider sense, need to be included in this wherever possible. Sharing responsibility for protection becomes part of the partnership contract. However, if family members are to feel that they have a partnership role in the child protection, then other partnership benefits become significant, in particular, a shared role in decision-making. This approach requires the worker to surrender professional dominance in decision-making. Realizing this paradigm shift can be difficult for workers, given the legacy of care practice in which professionals have always made the decisions. However, without the shift in philosophical approach to family, the danger remains, even within a participatory model, that decision-making will be weighted disproportionately toward the professionals.

Here we propose five central requirements for Effective Participatory Practice that address aspects of this paradigm shift. They also address some of the critical practice questions raised by the experience of using family decision-making in New Zealand, for example, issues of family isolation, structural power dynamics, and the management of complex or dangerous situations such as domestic violence and intergenerational sexual abuse. These five central requirements form the basis for participatory work with families, and will be discussed in detail. Chapter 7 will demonstrate how they may be operationalized within the casework setting.

1. Identifying Skills and Generating Hope

The first of EPP's central requirements is that of identifying skills and generating hope. Often, by the time they reach child protection services, families feel without hope, deskilled, undervalued, and sometimes quite desperate. Previous strategies for dealing with problems may have been tried and failed, and professional intervention may be feared and unwanted. The family may have experienced unsuccessful professional assistance, and lack confidence in a worker's ability to help a flagging and exhausted family system. In this context, generating hope can seem, in itself, a hopeless task. However, unless a family, and individuals within a family, can sense some possibility of future success, they will be unlikely to expend what is left of their depleted emotional resources on developing strategies for change. Hence, providing a sense of hope is an important component in the mobilization of the family's resources.

Within the EPP approach, hope is directly related to the family's *participation* in the process, rather than, necessarily, hopefulness with respect to outcome. This is an important distinction. Maintaining unrealistic hopes, for example, of a child's return to a parent, can be confusing and unhelpful. Some situations may never allow a child's return home. Hope, then, becomes more concretely connected with participation. Because of the familial ties, family have a right to have meaningful involvement in decision-making for the child. Unless this right is irrevocably withdrawn through the finality of adoption, it continues throughout the child's life. Indeed, developments toward more open adoption situations point to the increasing recognition of the lifelong importance of familial links and the significance of belonging with respect to adult well-being.

Having established the distinction between hope in terms of involvement and hopefulness with respect to outcome, we find that hope is fundamentally important to the change process. This notion is not a new one. In 1936, Rosenzweig considered factors that contribute to therapeutic effectiveness, and identified the worker's ability to inspire hope as a critical component to success. More recently, Jerome Frank's work on common factors that influence change has identified the arousal of hope and the restoration of morale as basic ingredients to successful outcomes in psychotherapy (Frank 1973, 1974, 1982). In order to understand how hope influences progress within a casework relationship, it is necessary to understand the factors that contribute to the generation of hope. These are: confidence, strength, reciprocity, and influence. The integration of these components provides the basis for early and ongoing work with the family (see Figure 6.2).

Confidence. Confidence is an important factor in the generation of hope. Worker confidence provides the first building block, and without it the hope edifice can crumble. Because participatory practice is predicated on family involvement, the worker needs to be enthusiastic about the centrality of this empowerment principle. A worker following this ap-

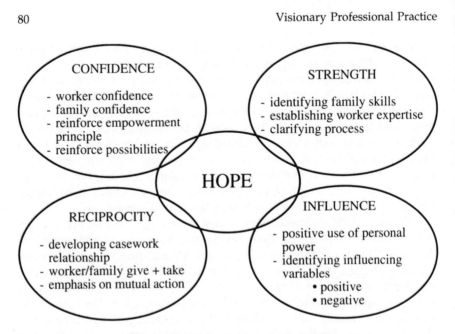

Figure 6.2. Theory of hope generation.

proach needs to have confidence that participatory practice can develop within the agency context, that is, that the agency is committed to the family involvement approach. As Croft and Beresford put it, "a more participatory practice is unlikely to be possible without more participatory agencies" (1994:58).

With respect to family, building their confidence in their ability to positively contribute can help generate hope. Clearly this goes hand in hand with the worker and agency commitment to the principle of empowerment. In these matters, families are very sensitive and attuned to tokenism. If a worker talks of participation and a sharing of decision-making but acts in ways that create doubt about his or her commitment to empowerment, then the family may have little investment in the process and may doubt the value of their contribution.

Strength. The second factor in the generation of hope is strength. Again, this can be considered from both the worker and the family perspective. Workers bring their knowledge, experience, and expertise to their practice. This is their strength. Establishing this strength and providing a sense that the worker has the skills and experience to be helpful to the family increases the potential for hope. The family also has strengths that contribute to this. It is the creative balance of worker and family strength that helps generate and maintain hope for both.

Reciprocity. The idea of developing a good casework relationship, or a positive therapeutic alliance, and the effect this has on outcome has been much discussed in the literature (Curtis 1991). Within the EPP approach, the emphasis is on the *reciprocity* of the relationship. Engaging family participation requires that there be an appreciation and acknowledgment of reciprocity within the worker/family relationship. This means mutual action, and practice give-and-take. Emphasizing mutual action from the early stages is a central principle of participatory practice, and is essential to the relationship building phase of the work. Trust is built around reciprocity, which then contributes to the worker/family sense of hope.

Influence. Although the use of influence may seem contradictory within the participatory approach, it is considered here as a factor that can contribute to the generation of hope. It is not necessarily popular to speak of the positive uses of power within the casework relationship. Because power can so easily be abused, social workers are sensitive to issues of power and may perceive their personal power as a negative factor in their work with families. It is true, of course, that power and power differentials have the potential for abusive manipulation when one is working with people. However, using one's influence positively can be an effective tool within the participatory approach. Recognizing, acknowledging, and harnessing personal influence, within the worker and family system, can be a powerful force for change.

While generating hope has the potential to influence motivation in the early and ongoing phases of the work, it is nevertheless only one factor of successful participatory practice. Goldfried (1991) argues that providing a sense of hope is little more than a promise that treatment is going to be helpful. While it may be an essential first step, it is insufficient alone to engender change. Within the participatory approach, part of generating hope also involves the identification of strengths, skills, and resources within the family. The adoption of a family strengths perspective is essential to this process. An important focus of the early work is the assessment of support systems and what is necessary to mobilize support. Acquiring information is part of skill development, and there are two sides to skill development in the participatory approach. First, identifying and supporting the skills already within the family, and second, providing additional information that will add to these skills (see Figure 6.3).

As discussed in Chapter 1, building on the family's strengths is not a new idea (Saleebey 1997), and is consistent with restorative methods of social work practice. Sharing information with families is also a familiar practice, but is reinforced here as a central requirement to a participatory

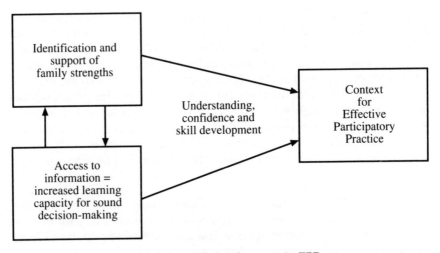

Figure 6.3. Skill development in EPP.

approach. Identifying skills and generating hope provides a basis for the family to begin the process of finding solutions, and is then a central requirement through ongoing phases of the work.

2. Blending Professional and Family Skills

The second central requirement of EPP is a context in which family and professional skills can be encouraged. In terms of family skills, the model is consistent with the competence-centered approach to family practice (Pecora et al. 1992). Again this requires the worker to support a family strengths perspective and to resist the many opportunities to develop professionally determined solutions. In this respect, participatory practice is easier said than done. Finding the balance between professional and family input is complex. At one end of the continuum are situations in which professional decision-making occurs. In this situation, family contribute little if anything toward the process and as a consequence may have minimal investment in solutions. At the other end of the continuum family decision-making exists in which the professional takes no part. Professional abandonment in the child protection context can result in dangerous situations for the vulnerable members of the family. Such professional abandonment can follow when workers feel deskilled in the face, perhaps, of family pressure. This can occur in the context of violent intimidation or, for example, when workers feel uncertain of the value of their professional input. This uncertainty may result from skill deficits, for example, in the cultural area, and can immobilize workers in terms of meeting their child protection mandate. Participatory practice occurs somewhere between these two extremes. It recognizes the value of both professional and family strengths, and is most likely to occur when workers recognize behavior falling around the two extremes (see Figure 6.4).

3. Managing Issues of Power in Family Systems and Family/Worker Systems

A sure way of undermining effective participatory practice is to neglect the significance of power dynamics within and across systems. Power dynamics within families can work positively to support family members individually, and to protect the interest of the family system as a whole. They can also work negatively. Some families have rigid role expectations that can result in a hierarchy of need satisfaction. The views and needs of the more dominant members of the family may become paramount, making it difficult for those less powerful to articulate their needs. Children's care and safety needs can be lost in the midst of this.

Effective Participatory Practice with family systems also requires that attention be paid to the power dynamic within the family/professional system. Because of their experience and expertise, professionals can be very influential in the problem-solving area of child protection. This is, of course, what they bring to the partnership. Using professional knowledge and expertise to further the aims of participatory practice becomes the challenge for workers as they avoid the many opportunities to take the problem-solving lead.

Power dynamics across worker systems may also negatively influence participatory practice. When families get stuck, the problem does not always rest within the family system alone. It could be based in the worker/family system, or could be negatively influenced by the wider system, either arising from interagency or interdisciplinary conflict. An awareness of the complexities of worker dynamics is a necessary precursor to the acknowledgment and addressing of such negative influence.

→		←
Increased professional input	more equal blending of family and professional input	Increased family input
Professional abandonment - minimal professional involvement - increased potential for risk	= optimum conditions for effective participatory practice	Professional decision-making - minimal family involvement - decreased investment potential

Figure 6.4. Balancing family and worker input into decision-making.

4. Protecting Vulnerable Members

Working through complex family issues within the EPP approach depends on the views of all family members being heard and considered. Family members need to feel able to contribute without fear of intimidation or harm. Because the worker is using family collectively as a solution resource, he or she has a responsibility to ascertain and address the safety needs of those involved. Given that violence and intimidation are frequently factors that characterize families that come to the notice of protective agencies, there is every chance that these factors will be present during the phases of work. Workers need to be vigilant to this.

5. Empowering and Encouraging Participatory Practice

The fifth central requirement of EPP has to do with embracing and giving effect to the empowerment principles of participatory practice. Empowerment models of social work practice provide an important theoretical and philosophical framework within which participatory practice occurs. The dichotomy of powerlessness and action is of essential importance within the EPP approach. Taking action is the antithesis of powerlessness. If it is accepted that taking action to resolve family problems results in agency over outcomes, then if the family provide solutions there is an increased likelihood that they will have greater investment in outcomes. The outcomes become theirs. If the professional makes the decisions and provides the solutions, the professional has a greater investment in the outcome. Unfortunately such professional investment does not always provide the best incentive for client change. An awareness of the powerlessness/action dichotomy then and the use of professional expertise to further participatory practice are critical components of the approach.

The five central requirements described above provide what we consider to be the basis for participatory practice in the child care and protection field. Within the participatory approach attention is paid to them at each phase of the work. In this way, as work progresses, the worker can check back with the family to ensure that the requirements are being met. In order to do this, the work must always be *transparent* to the family. Through all phases of the work, the worker needs to ensure that the family understands the rationale behind the participatory approach, and how this impacts upon the decision-making processes. Having outlined the central requirements to participatory practice, we will now consider how they may be operationalized in practice.

7

Harnessing Strengths, Achieving Partnerships: Operationalizing EPP's Central Requirements

This chapter presents the potential EPP action steps that evolve from the five central requirements described in Chapter 5. These steps are designed to provide multiple pathways to the achievement of participatory practice, and guidelines for the development of decision-making processes. The following issues are discussed:

- Phases of Effective Participatory Practice
- Facilitating family involvement, family support systems, and the professional/family partnership in decision-making
- Anticipating problems; developing solutions
- Maintaining solution-based momentum
- Identifying achievement indicators

Within the EPP model, there are three phases of work: the preliminary phase, the participatory phase, and the review/follow-up phase. The participatory phase is modeled on the Family Group Conference process of family decision-making, which was first established in New Zealand law with the introduction of the Children, Young Persons and their Families Act of 1989, and described in detail in Chapter 2. However, while it could be argued that the FGC process is the most significant and central innovation within the legislation, EPP reinforces the importance of the preliminary and follow-up phases as critical to the achievement of sound decision-making. The EPP model surrounds the participatory phase with the preparatory and review phases, and ties these concretely to the EPP central requirements (see Figure 7.1).

The preliminary phase is critical to the success of the participatory phase. If the family and workers are ill-prepared for the FGC, at best the participatory vision of the process can be undermined; at worst the participatory phase itself can be damaging to individuals and/or the family group as a whole. Equally, EPP reinforces the importance of the review/follow-up phase. Without strong emphasis on review and support, the sometimes fragile decisions made at the FGC can falter and the impetus for ongoing change be lost. Hence, within EPP the participatory phase cannot stand alone and is only effective when supported by the other two phases.

Returning to the five EPP central requirements then, we will now discuss how these are operationalized. The model works by the systematic unfolding of the central requirements into action steps, and there are action steps in each of the three phases of the work (Table 7.1). However, it is important to note that the model provides *suggestions* for action steps, and that these can be modified and developed to fit the unique circumstances of each family. The model has, therefore, the scope within it to be adapted as necessary.

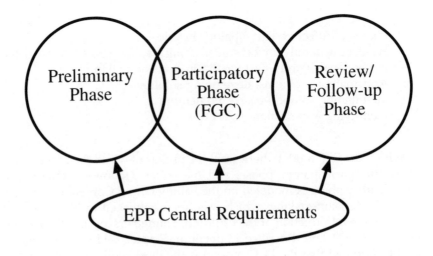

Figure 7.1. Phases of Effective Participatory Practice.

EPP PRELIMINARY PHASE

In terms of the first EPP central requirement—identifying skills and generating hope—the preliminary phase of the model is characterized by meetings with parents, family, and family support systems. Prefatory sessions with parents are valuable in assessing the extent of the necessary preliminary work. Early discussions may reveal family tensions that require attention before decision-making can occur during the participatory phase. Introducing a discussion of the model's central requirements can provide a basis for understanding, and reinforces the concept of family solution-based work. It is important that the vision and process of the work is transparent (see Figure 7.2).

Families will not necessarily be used to having a participatory role when working with professionals. By making the central principles transparent in the early phase of the work, individuals in the family can be encouraged to begin to construct their responses in terms of individual involvement in the context of family-based solutions. Just as workers have had to make a paradigm shift from professional decision-making to family decision-making, the family have to make a similar shift. The worker needs to be able to communicate EPP's central requirements in a language accessible to the family. What is necessary is a meeting of meaning. The basis of EPP, and its central requirements, need to make sense to the family, so that the purpose of their involvement is also clear and considered to be an essential component to the process of decision-making.

With regard to identifying family skills, undertaking a comprehensive genealogy can be particularly useful. It can also help to identify potential conflicts. Much has been written about the value of using genograms and ecomaps in family work (Barker 1986). Such tools can provide an enormous amount of information very quickly and can provide important data, not only with respect to who is in the family, but also who is significant to the family and who is lost from it. Using a genogram that can be added to is particularly helpful. Different family members can identify where the gaps are in family information, and building the genealogy can provide support as the strengths within the family become more apparent.

An assessment of cultural needs is also an important part of the preliminary phase. In this discussion we use the term *culture* broadly to include religion, affectional preference, and family culture as well as ethnic culture. Because culture plays such a significant part in family and family/professional dynamics, and because cultural skills within the family have

Table 7.1. Effective Participatory Practice

		Potential EPP Action Steps		
EPP Central Requirements	Preliminary phase		Participatory phase: FGC	Review/follow-up phase
1. Identifying skills and generating hope	1. Preliminary meetings with parents • assessment of necessary preliminary work • discussion of EPP central requirements • comprehensive genealogy 2. Cultural needs assessment • consultants identified as required 3. Preliminary meetings with family and/or support • assessment of preliminary work required • further develop genealogy • discussion of EPP central requirements 4. Submeetings as required		1. Begin with appropriate cultural protocol 2. FGC process, aims, and goals discussed 3. EPP central requirements reiterated 4. Family problem-solving skills encouraged	1. Ensure ongoing support to FGC plans 2. Be alert and monitor commitment to and frustration with plans and support as required 3. Support family safety plan for child 4. Maintain appropriate casework relationship
2. Blending professional and family skills	1. Prelim meeting with workers • discussion of EPP central requirements • identification of possible philosophical/practice conflicts • identification and		1. Full worker/case information shared 2. Family encouraged to question and clarify 3. Shared decision-making concept promoted 4. Facilitate agreement between worker and	1. In casework practice, maintain balance of worker/family input re: safety care plan 2. Monitor maintenance of professional support service 3. Facilitate worker, family,

		family to safety care plan	and/or worker/family meetings as required
	discussion of family skills • resolve worker conflict 2. Identify cultural supports		
3. Managing issues of power in family systems and family/worker systems	1. Submeetings of critical individuals, diads, etc. e.g., women, support team 2. Discussion of complexities of family and family/worker dynamics	1. Encourage participation from all members 2. Enable views to be expressed by proxy if necessary 3. Explore range of ways in which views may be expressed 4. Avoid worker domination of process	1. Encourage dialogue re: positive implication of FGC plans 2. Initiate submeetings as necessary
4. Protecting vulnerable members	1. Identification of safety issues 2. Establishment of support systems 3. Submeetings to establish safety support plan	1. Facilitate implementation of safety support plan 2. Be cognisant of power dynamics during conference 3. Intervene if necessary 4. Ensure protection in planning and review phase	1. Maintain support of safety support plan 2. Maintain ongoing dialogue re: safety 3. Initiate submeetings as necessary
5. Empowering and encouraging participatory practice	1. Individuals prepared for FDM process 2. Family prepared for FDM process 3. Encourage thinking around need for services 4. Discourage premature adoption of professional strategies and plans	1. Ensure opportunity for private family deliberation 2. Encourage family problem-resolution skills and potential redevelopment of plan 3. Ensure availability of information for family 4. Provide for family/client determined time frame 5. Attend to cultural protocols	1. Encourage family monitoring of safety care plan and support as necessary 2. Encourage families determined contact with worker

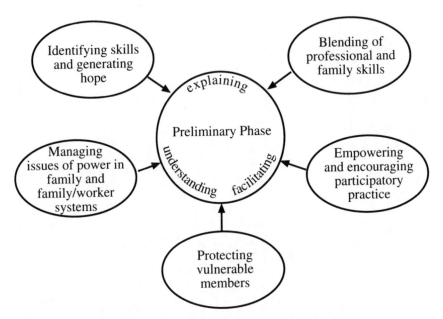

Figure 7.2. Making the vision of Effective Participatory Practice transparent.

the potential to enhance decision-making processes, it is important
to harness these strengths. During the process of the work, cultural
strengths within the family may begin to emerge. There may be people
within the family who are able to undertake the role of interpreter or
cultural adviser. Recognizing and discussing the issue of culture and
family protocol can encourage the family to determine their own cultural
processes and this helps to avoid worker insensitivity in this area. Again,
the aim is to find a meeting of meaning, a way through the process of
decision-making that can respect and enhance both family and worker
strengths. When a worker struggles to find such a meeting of meaning,
the use of a cultural consultant is another way of working through what
can sometimes seem a cultural minefield. If a cultural consultant is engaged, it is also important to spend time with that person talking through
the central requirements of EPP, for example, the third central requirement. Managing issues of power in family systems and family/worker
systems could potentially present difficulties if a meeting of meaning is
not found cross-culturally. If a worker's aim is to facilitate a process of
participation, it needs to fit within the family's framework of understanding. It needs to make sense to the family and individuals within the
family. This is not to say that some family values cannot be challenged,

but that cultural belief systems need to be worked with rather than fought against.

Prefatory sessions with parents are followed by a similar pattern of work with extended family and support persons (see Figure 7.3). As such, the work unfolds to reveal the developing safety support network for the child. Sessions with extended family and support persons are designed to further illuminate problem-solving potential within the family system and to generate support for the child and immediate family. Wherever possible, facilitating meetings between family members and family support people will help to prepare the ground for the participatory phase of the process.

The second of the central requirements relates to the blending of professional and family skills. Troubled families who come to the attention of protective services often have many professionals involved in their lives. When services are well coordinated, open communication and frequent liaison across worker systems can enhance work with families. Unfortunately, services in the child protection field are often poorly coordinated, and because of the emphasis on family involvement in the EPP approach, problems can arise if workers experience philosophical and practice conflicts. One cannot assume a degree of accord among workers. Indeed, it is not unusual to find differences of opinion concerning the need for family participation, particularly when the parent is the perpetrator of abuse. Again, it is important to find a meeting of meaning, and in the preliminary phase to identify any philosophical or practice tensions

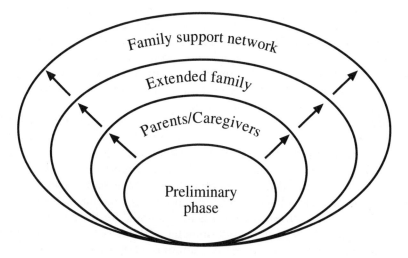

Figure 7.3. The unfolding of the child's safety support network.

between workers. It is not helpful if they emerge during the participatory phase of the process. A thorough discussion of the EPP central requirements and a discussion of family strengths is a step toward identifying these. For example, if one of the contributing workers comes from an agency supporting alternative care as the preferred option for children at risk, it is important to work through the possible influence this might have on the process of decision-making. As previously mentioned, finding the balance between professional and family input into decision-making can be complex. However, if such tensions remain undetected, there is an increased likelihood that the spirit and process of participatory practice will be undermined.

Managing issues of power in family systems and family/worker systems is the third central requirement of EPP. During the preliminary phase, discussions to identify issues of power are critical to the strengthening of participatory practice. If domestic violence characterizes a couple relationship, it is unwise, if not impossible to address child protection issues without addressing other aspects of family violence. Participatory practice cannot exist when a partner is so intimidated by threats of violence that he or she is unable to contribute. That said, anyone who has worked with domestic violence will attest to the difficulties and frustrations experienced in managing power and violence in couple relationships. Within the participatory approach, the power of the group becomes the important factor in dealing with violence. The experts on family violence can be found in the families themselves. Bringing the women together to talk about the issue of male violence within the family can generate supports hitherto unidentified within the family system and can directly attack the conspiracy of silence that too often characterizes this kind of abuse. Bringing the men of the family together can also have potential in terms of confronting familial violence. This work must be done carefully and requires skilled intervention. It is, however, a central part of the necessary work within the participatory approach and workers must have access to training on family violence if they are to undertake work in the child protection area.

Inextricably linked with this is the fourth central requirement of EPP, the protection of vulnerable members involved in the child protection process. Inevitably, confronting abusive situations will raise conflicts and tensions in families. Sometimes, families are supportive of members as the issues are worked through. At other times, however, family members are scapegoated as alliances develop and family members take sides. Such alienation significantly prevents the potential for the person to participate in the processes of decision-making, and if it exists, it is important that the worker facilitate the establishment of support systems. Early in the preliminary phase it is also necessary to identify safety issues for family members, and to establish a safety support plan. Part of the work involves building alliances within the family, including the extended family and wider network.

Operationalizing the fifth central requirement—empowering and encouraging participatory practice—requires that family members be fully prepared for the decision-making processes that are to follow. Checks of the family's understanding of the process will indicate to the worker whether the family is sufficiently prepared. For example, do family members know who will be involved in the process? Do they understand the role of professionals? Do they understand the reasons for involving wider family and support systems? Do they feel sufficiently supported going into the participatory phase?

For families who have been long-term recipients of welfare help, the concept of participatory practice may be very different from their previous experiences. They may seek solutions from professionals, and may doubt their own ability to contribute to the decision-making process. In these circumstances, setting the basis for family participation can begin by encouraging them to think about the need for services, and the kind of help that might best suit their situation. In addition, the family can be discouraged from the premature adoption of professional strategies and plans.

The purpose of the preliminary phase is to prepare the ground for effective participatory practice. It needs to be undertaken thoroughly and can be time-consuming. It is important that the preliminary phase not be hurried because of safety concerns for the child. If there are safety concerns, these must be attended to in the first instance. No child should be left at risk while waiting for the work to be undertaken.

EPP PARTICIPATORY PHASE

The participatory phase is modeled on the FGC intervention strategy that originated in New Zealand in 1989 (Connolly 1994). To briefly recap, the FGC was established in law and formalized a developing change in social work practice that embraced processes of family decision-making. When a child is identified as being in need of care and protection, the FGC process brings together members of the family to discuss and problem-solve the child protection issues. In addition to the immediate family, members of the extended family are also invited to the FGC, so that the support and problem-solving capacities of the wider family network can be utilized.

The FGC and EPP models share central principles that include an emphasis on the protection of the child, the strengthening of the stability of the family, cultural relevancy, and a commitment to partnership in decision-making. As such, the participatory phase meeting(s) begin with a welcome appropriate to the cultural protocol of the ethnic group involved, an articulation of the principles outlined above, and a reiteration of EPP's central requirements. Discussion is encouraged and the notion of the family being an active participant in decision-making is reinforced. Like the FGC process, the EPP participatory phase has three stages: information sharing, private deliberation by the family, and agreement between family and professionals.

At all stages, EPP's central requirements must be considered. In restating the first two central requirements—identifying skills and generating hope, and blending professional and family skills—the worker builds on the notion that the family has problem-solving skills, and that these can be brought together in a shared decision-making process. The goal of the participatory phase is that a safety care plan for the child be established, emerging from the shared resource of the family and professional group. In order to make sound decisions the family needs to have all the information available, and it is necessary for workers to share information regarding the investigation and other relevant aspects of the social work intervention. In order for the family to make decisions, they require all the benefits of the professionals' expertise. This is important in terms of the blending of professional and family skills. Not only do the family require information about the investigation, but also relevant information with respect to the specific nature of the difficulties within the family.

For example, if it is a situation of sexual abuse, then the family needs to have information about the etiology of sexual abuse, patterns of offender behavior, victim response, and impact of abuse on the child and the wider family system. If drug and/or alcohol abuse is part of the problem within the family, then the worker needs to advise the family on aspects of drug and alcohol abuse: indicators, treatment, and prognosis issues and how this impacts on, for example, parenting. Hence, the expert body of knowledge can help the family to better assess risk, and by sharing professional expertise the basis for shared decision-making is also established.

By the time the participatory phase is reached, it is hoped that strategies will be in place from the previous phase to manage issues of power as work progresses. It is important that all members of the family be encouraged to participate. Preliminary work may have revealed reluctance on the part of some family members to speak or contribute their opinion during decision-making meetings. In these situations, it is necessary to explore the range of ways in which views may be expressed, for example by proxy. Managing issues of power also means avoiding processes that are dominated by individuals or factions within the meeting. That said, the way in which this is managed will inevitably differ from family to family. The way in which power dynamics are managed in a Samoan family situation may well look different from their management in a family of European origin. Managing power dynamics within a closed religious community might be different from nonreligious families. While we reinforce the need to attend to power dynamics, this must be done in a way that is meaningful and tractable for the family.

Early work to identify and support vulnerable members of the family by this stage should have resulted in the development of a safety support plan. This can be monitored by the facilitator, who must also be vigilant to potential undermining during the conference. In bringing people together, the facilitator has a responsibility to ensure that vulnerable members at the meeting are protected. Even with the best of planning, unexpected dynamics can emerge, and it may be necessary to intervene, or even put the meeting into recess while these issues are attended to.

The empowering exigency of EPP's fifth central requirement supports the notion of family having the opportunity to deliberate in private. Private deliberation, without professional involvement, directly encourages participatory practice. It provides the opportunity for family members to challenge each other without the pressure of professional oversight and to formulate plans that are realistic for them. Having reinforced the importance of private deliberation for the family, it is also important that the worker take steps to ensure the safety of family members during the process. Hopefully, the potential for abusive dynamics will have been identified during the preliminary stage of the work, and strategies developed to manage these concerns. Private family deliberations should not exclude support persons for those more vulnerable and can be included in the development of the safety support plan. If, finally, it is the workers' assessment that the private deliberations would compromise the safety of participants, then thought should be given to the involvement of an independent mediator who could manage this part of the process.

In order for the family to make sound decisions, it is necessary for them to have the time and resources to do so. This means that the facilitator must ensure that any additional information the family needs is made available and that sufficient time is given for them to arrive at decisions. This can sometimes cause frustrations for the worker. However, within reason, family determined time-frames are an important feature of the participatory approach.

Agreement to plans and decisions follows the private deliberation stage of the participatory phase. In Chapter 6, we spoke of the importance of balancing family and worker input into decision-making, and the need to avoid the two extremes of professional abandonment and professional decision-making. This is never more important than in the agreement stage of EPP. Generally, practice experience indicates that given the opportunity and enough information, families are keen to make decisions that provide support and safety for the child. Rarely would decisions be made that leave a child knowingly at risk. More frequently, it is the questions around how support and safety can be ensured that require negotiation between the family and the workers. For example, if it is decided that counseling is necessary, then what type and who pays could be the focus of the negotiation. If a child is to be placed with family members, resourcing issues may emerge and also, perhaps, the need for legal sanctions. In this respect, the worker has a brokerage role, and the need for the worker to have good information on community services and resources cannot be understated.

EPP REVIEW/FOLLOW-UP PHASE

During the review/follow-up phase, it is critical that the family be supported as they work on the plans and decisions made during the participatory phase. Enthusiasm may wax and wane as the hard work continues, and maintaining a sense of hope is an important aspect of the ongoing work. Often the family is buoyed up and enthusiastic at the time of the conference. It is important to recognize, however, that decisions can be fragile. They need nurturing and strengthening as time goes on. Decisions that appeared easy, sensible, and manageable at the time of the meeting might become a complex struggle in the reality of day-to-day living. The worker needs to closely monitor family commitment to the plans and be alert to and supportive of family as they become frustrated with the pace of change or seeming lack of progress. Maintaining regular contact is important. In many ways, once decisions are made, a child is considered safe and a plan is set in place, it is tempting for a worker to breathe a sigh of relief and go on to the next family. After all, there always seems to be another family needing attention in child protection work. But maintenance effort during the review/follow-up phase can prove to be a resource well utilized. If a plan breaks down, it can be difficult to recapture the initial enthusiasm, both from a worker and family perspective. A supportive casework relationship is necessary not only to family morale, but also in terms of the blending of family and professional skills. In casework practice, it is important to try to strike an appropriate balance of worker and family input. Too much worker involvement may result in less energy and commitment from the family. Equally, too little may result in a delayed response to important cues, and the undermining of the safety care plan(s).

The review phase is characterized also by its ongoing attention to the management of power issues within the family and family/professional systems. The spirit and intent of family decisions can be undermined if they lack the support of people within the professional support network, or within the family itself. Here the coordination of professional services is crucial. Because workers in the child protection field are often under-resourced and because the need for protective services continues to increase, professional networking and liaison can be neglected. When workers have busy caseloads and minimal time for liaison, the potential for worker miscommunications is increased. This can sometimes result in a worker thinking that another worker is providing support and monitoring, when, in fact, nobody is. Ongoing dialogue across the worker systems is important to avoid such misunderstandings and to monitor safety support plans for the child and family members. Ongoing dialogue is also important with respect to power issues within the family.

The emphasis on empowerment in the participatory approach supports the idea that the family, and individuals within the family, have the major role in the monitoring of safety care plans. Primarily, the role of the professional is one of supporter and facilitator. This is not to say, of course, that the professional has no responsibility with respect to child safety. Rather, the safety of the child is a shared responsibility between the family and the worker. Family monitoring of the child's safety care plan has a number of advantages. First, it is likely to be more regular than professional monitoring and involve frequent sighting of the child. Second, because of the nature of familial relationships, the child may be less likely to hide from a trusted family member any problems that may emerge. Adults in the family may also be more prepared to talk to family members about frustrations they may have with the child, or with the safety care plan, whereas they may fear ramifications of such discussions with professionals. In supporting the role of family in the monitoring of child safety, the worker might usefully encourage family-determined contact with the worker. This reinforces the idea once again that the maintenance of a safety support network (which includes workers) is a shared responsibility. A more equal balance of responsibility can also have the effect of increasing the family's agency over the process.

In using the EPP model, workers are encouraged to identify their own action steps within each phase of the process. Families are different, and the way in which families respond to working through EPP's central requirements may also be different. In developing the model we do not want to limit a worker's potential with regard to developing creative processes. Nor do we want to prescribe steps to be used with every family

Table 7.2 Effective Participatory Practice

| | | EPP Achievement Indicators | |
EPP Central Requirements	Preliminary phase	Participatory phase: FGC	Review/follow-up phase
1. Identifying skills and generating hope	1. Preliminary work identified and family engaged 2. Genealogy completed 3. EPP central requirements discussed and understood 4. Context for 2nd stage development established	1. Cultural protocols attended to 2. Necessary information communicated to family providing basis for sound decision-making 3. Optimum condition for development of family problem solving skills provided	1. Contact with family and extended family maintained 2. Family advised of progress 3. Family provided with support as required 4. Casework relationship established
2. Blending professional and family skills	1. Workers provided with opportunity to discuss EPP central requirement 2. Philosophical/practice conflicts discussed and resolved 3. Family strengths identified 4. Cultural supports identified	1. Family receives full information from workers 2. Questioning/clarifying context achieved 3. Statements made promoting shared decision-making 4. Positive faciliation of agreement to plans	1. Balance of worker/family input into safety care plan demonstrated 2. Professional support available when necessary 3. Meetings held as appropriate

3. Managing issues of power in family systems and family/worker systems	1. Power dynamics identified and assessed 2. Dynamics discussed as appropriate 3. Strategies developed to manage power issues	1. All members given opportunity to participate 2. Balance achieved re worker/family input 3. Where necessary, creative ways found for expression of views	1. Dialogue open re positive implementation of FGC plans 2. Submeetings initiated as required
4. Protecting vulnerable members	1. Safety issues identified and documented 2. Identification of support system if necessary 3. Safety support plan identified and discussed	1. Vulnerable family members protected 2. Worker identifies and attends to negative power dynamics	1. Support system maintained and submeetings initiated as required
5. Empowering and encouraging participatory practice	1. Parents preparedness for FGC checked 2. Family preparedness for FGC checked	1. Family have opportunity to deliberate privately 2. Family provided with support when necessary 3. Family-determined time-frame for process 4. Families encouraged to find own solutions	1. Family satisfied with safety care plan and monitoring role 2. Family responsive to contact maintenance with worker

that comes to the attention of protective services. Rather, the action steps identified in Table 7.1 will, we hope, provide some *ideas* of how the central requirements can be operationalized within the casework setting, and may be used as a key to exploring the unique experiences of each family.

EPP ACHIEVEMENT INDICATORS

In addition to the maintenance and review of family decisions, part of the EPP model includes the identification of achievement indicators at each stage of the preliminary, participation, and review/follow-up phases (see Table 7.2).

Again the model's central requirements are used as a framework. For example, with respect to the first central requirement—identifying skills and generating hope—the preliminary phase achievement indicators may include whether the extent of the preliminary work has been identified and whether the family has been engaged in the participatory process. The completion of a genealogy may be another achievement indicator, and whether or not the model's central requirements have been discussed and understood. Each phase of the model has a set of achievement indicators that are concretely tied to the central requirements, and

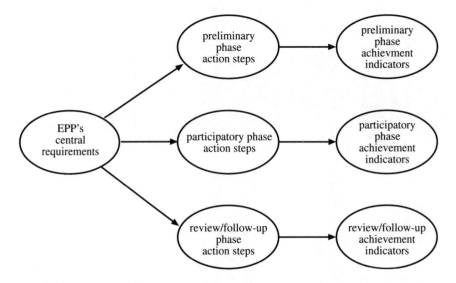

Figure 7.4. The developing process of Effective Participatory Practice.

are best used to review the phase as the worker and family move through the process. Reviewing each phase in this way offers insight into the progress of the phase and whether the family is ready to move on, for example, from the preliminary to the participatory phase. Reviewing achievement indicators is an important part of the EPP model. It provides an opportunity to reflect on practice, and to consider the unique differ ences of each family. As with the EPP action steps, workers are encouraged to develop their own achievement indicators as work with each family unfolds. The EPP action steps are informed by the central requirements, and the achievement indicators emerge from the action steps, and so the process develops (see Figure 7.4).

Working in partnership with family in the child protection area can be complex and difficult work. Involving family in decision-making, while offering the potential to significantly increase the protective safety net around the child, also raises issues that must be considered if positive outcomes are to be found for children at risk. The EPP model provides an integrated framework for understanding and working with the complex dynamics of family participatory practice. Chapter 8 will demonstrate, with the use of case studies, how the process of decision-making is made possible by the application of the EPP model.

8

Effective Participatory Practice in Action

This chapter develops further the EPP model with an action section. It uses casework examples to illuminate the processes of decision-making made possible by the application of the model, and highlights the particular tensions inherent in participatory practice. The chapter will explore:

- The illustration of theory and practice integration
- Particular complexities within the participatory approach
- The development of professional and family skills

In this book we have proposed five central requirements for Effective Participatory Practice. We suggest that they can be explored with each family for whom a family decision-making process is considered. Here we will demonstrate, by use of two case studies, how these can be integrated into practice with families in child protection. The case studies have been chosen to illustrate the complexities of two particular family situations that can represent a challenge to participatory practice: domestic violence situations and the isolated family for whom there is no network of extended family support. Inevitably, using a participatory approach toward decision-making will be easier with some families than with others. In exploring the more difficult cases, we hope to attend to some of the practice issues raised when seemingly intractable family situations occur, and where cooperation with family seems impossible because of the very nature of the problems faced.

In each instance, we will first present the case study situation and then use the model to explore how the participatory process could develop. This will be based on the EPP action steps chart presented in Chapter 7, and modified for the families discussed. Attention will be paid to the preliminary and participatory phases of the work, and a discussion of issues will follow each action sheet.

CASE STUDY 1: THE CRAIG FAMILY

Mr. and Mrs. Craig have been referred following allegations of Mr. Craig's abuse of his son Billy, aged six. This is not the first time Billy has come to notice. The school has previously expressed concerns to protective services. A medical examination has shown that Billy has extensive bruising to his upper body and he has a fracture of the left arm. He has been placed in an emergency foster home. Preliminary discussions with Mr. and Mrs. Craig suggest that there is reason to believe that Mr. Craig has also been violent toward his wife and their daughter, Tania, aged thirteen. Mr. Craig presents as an extremely angry, belligerent, and intimidating man. Mrs. Craig has sought refuge on two occasions following physical abuse; however, on both occasions she has returned to the family home without taking any formal action against her husband. Exploration of the family network reveals that the maternal extended family are supportive, particularly the maternal grandmother and Mrs. Craig's sister. The paternal extended family have lost touch with Mr. Craig in recent years; however, Mr. Craig's sister lives locally and has indicated an interest in the welfare of the children.

EPP Preliminary Phase: The Craig family

Table 8.1 provides the general action steps that may be used with all families, followed by action steps that are specific to the Craig family throughout the preliminary phase. The areas of professional skill development and family skill development have been delineated.

Discussion: The Preliminary Phase with the Craig Family

The purpose of the preliminary phase with the Craig family is to prepare the ground for optimum individual and family participation throughout all stages of the work. Because of the abusive nature of the Craigs' relationship, particular attention needs to be paid to managing issues of power and developing a context within which all members of the family can participate. To do this, the workers need to be knowledgeable about and skilled in dealing with abusive couple and family dynamics. The preliminary phase provides an opportunity for an assessment of the skills and experience of the workers involved in the process, and the building of specialist knowledge where necessary. When unfamiliar with an area of practice it is not unusual to consult with professional experts in the field. Just as workers may engage cultural advisors when confronted with unfamiliar cultural situations, it is also important to draw on the expert knowledge of professionals in the domestic violence field when confronted by family violence. When working in the area of family violence it is also important that systems of worker support and supervision be established. If individuals are violent, creating fear and apprehension, the potential for collusive practice is increased. Fear and intimidation can result in the worker adopting a more permissive response to the abuser, and monitoring worker response is one way of minimizing the potential for collusive practice. Here the role of the supervisor or co-worker is a critical one. Together the worker and the supervisor can develop strategies for monitoring and managing family and worker responses to violence.

With respect to the family, workers need to identify oppressive power dynamics and develop strategies for dealing with these dynamics as they undermine the participatory process. In this particular case scenario, the family had a history of domestic violence reportings, and so it was possible for the worker to explore the issues more fully with both Mr. and Mrs. Craig. In some situations, however, domestic violence may he hidden and the worker needs to be alert to its potential when violence characterizes parent/child interactions. Child protection experience and training does not always consider the potential for child abuse to be a connected branch of a wider family violence problem. Indeed, the special needs and safety concerns of the mothers of abused children can sometimes be, if not ignored, certainly underestimated within the child protection context. Abused women can be neglected, *and* given the added responsibility to provide for the safety needs of children. In this situation, Mrs. Craig's position within the family needs to be carefully considered and her interests protected. In all cases where violence characterizes a family's dynamic, the need for safety support plans should be assessed. Both Mrs. Craig and Tania may need safety support, and it is important that their needs be identified and strategies for providing protection established. Drawing upon the strengths of the family "experts" can be useful when working with violence. For example, bringing the women in the family together to explore ways in which family members may participate taps into family strengths and can build alliances. Alliances may also be found across family boundaries. Potential support from family

Table 8.1 EPP Preliminary Phase: Case Study 1: The Craig Family

EPP Central Requirements	General EPP Action Steps (to be considered with all families)	Specific Considerations: The Craig Family	
		Development of Professional Skills	Development of family skills

1. Identifying skills and generating hope	1. Preliminary meetings with parents
	  * assessment of necessary prelim work
	  * discussion of EPP central requirements
	  * comprehensive genealogy
	2. Cultural needs assessment
	  * consultants identified as required
	3. Preliminary meetings with family and/or support
	  * assessment of preliminary work required
	  * further develop genealogy
	  * discussion of EPP central requirements
	4. Submeetings as required
		* Development of professional knowledge of abusive couple and family dynamics
		* Assess necessity for training
		* Consult/liaise with professionals in domestic violence field
		* Engage consultants if appropriate
		* Establish systems of support and supervision for workers
			* Identify areas of support and expertise within family, particularly family violence 'experts'
			* Begin process of building network of support for Mrs. Craig within and outside family
			* Provide reassurance with respect to safety during process of the work

2. Blending professional and family skills	1. Preliminary meetings with workers
	  * discussion of EPP central requirements
	  * identification of possible philosophical/practice conflicts
		* Identify professionals working with family and expert knowledge areas required
		* Explore ways of sharing knowledge with family, e.g., abuse dynamics
			* Work with diads and groups of family 'experts'
			* Facilitate discussions of family strategies for dealing with abusive dynamics
			* Link family with other community resources

	* identification and discussion of family skills * resolve worker conflict 2. Identify cultural supports	understanding; services available * Expand community links with self-help groups and family education programs	* Explore potential for the development of safety support plans
3. Managing issues of power in family systems and family/worker systems	1. Submeetings of critical individuals, diads, etc. e.g., women, support team, etc 2. Discussion of complexities of family and family/worker dynamics	* Identify oppressive power dynamics within family * Discuss dynamics with supervisor/consultants * Develop strategies for helping family clarification of abuse dynamics * Develop system for monitoring worker and family response to oppressive dynamics	* Encourage clarification of alliances and power dynamics in submeetings * Begin exploration of views re FGC attendance * Facilitate ideas re need for and development of safety support plans * Begin mobilization of family system supports
4. Protecting vulnerable members	1. Identification of safety issues 2. Establishment of support systems 3. Submeetings to establish safety support plan	* Identify family members needing safety support, e.g., Mrs. Craig, Tania * Generate worker strategies for providing protection through preliminary and participatory phases * Clarify attendance re FGC	* Discuss process of participatory phase * Clarify safety support system and plan * Identify protective strategies
5. Empowering and encouraging participatory practice	1. Individuals prepared for FDM process 2. Family prepared for FDM process 3. Encourage thinking around need for services 4. Discourage premature adoption of professional strategies and plans	* Workers prepared and cognizant of potential oppression and/or retaliatory dynamics * Bottom lines re safety issues during process clarified * Arrangements established for worker support during FGC process	* Individual family members have identified supports during process * Strategies developed for participatory process by all family members

friends and community resource persons can be explored and encouraged in the development of safety support systems.

With respect to the role of the professional during the preliminary phase, the emphasis is on preparation; the preparatory work in bringing together a potentially hostile and aggressive group, and the management of the group once together. It is important that the family, and its individual members, understand the process of the family group conference (FGC): what they might expect from it and how much support they can expect from the worker. During the preliminary phase, decisions are made with respect to when the FGC will be held, and who should attend. The legislation in New Zealand that underpins the FGC clearly promotes the involvement of all family in the decision-making process. However, as discussed in Chapter 2, the legislation also gives the coordinator sweeping powers of exclusion, so that individuals can be excluded from the FGC if it is considered that their presence would be detrimental to the decision-making process. A litmus test with respect to attendance is whether the conference provides for the safety needs of the people involved, and whether safety is undermined by the presence of any individual. Although participatory practice rests upon the notions of partnership and cooperation, there will clearly be times when it is not possible or desirable to bring together the whole family. It is essential that principles do not override safety. Domestic violence is about the silencing of voices. Communication of suppression is subtle and can be easily overlooked by workers in family practice. While family decision-making has a place in child protection, if wife / partner battering is identified it is important that gender-specific prefatory work be undertaken with the couple before bringing them to the decision-making forum. Recent work in the area of profeminist couple and family therapy can be useful to workers confronted by family violence in the child protection area. Trute (1998) offers a framework for understanding the dynamics of violence work with couples, and although he is writing about therapeutic services, the principles underpinning his work have significance also within child protection practice. In both situations, couple dynamics that are characterized by intimidation and fear do not provide a context in which both partners can freely express their concerns. Unless the violence can be explicitly discussed as an aspect of the couple dynamic at the FGC, there can be little hope of hearing the voice of the abused woman, or indeed, protecting her interests more generally. Child protection issues are contextual and cannot be separated from wider family violence issues. Hence, the use of family decision-making models must be timed to ensure that family members are not placed at further risk.

If the family group conference is to go ahead, there are different ways in which individual family members' participation can be effected. The process of participation may, indeed, include attending decision-making meetings. Or maybe if attendance is not possible, alternative ways of communicating the views of some family members need to be found. Although not ideal, there have been situations where two meetings have been held concurrently when hostility within the family has prevented the possibility of having one decision-making forum. This has occurred when the man has been violent and the couple were estranged and would not consider being in the same room together. Case situations that are characterized by domestic violence or intergenerational sexual abuse are probably the most problematic with regard to this. Workers need to know as much as possible about the family dynamics before planning the participatory phase, and each family situation will demand its own participatory strategy. In this case scenario, because there was an acknowledgment of family violence and Mr. Craig had agreed to go into treatment, the FGC proceeded with all family members in attendance.

EPP Participatory Phase (FGC): The Craig Family

The participatory phase, or the Family Group Conference, is the opportunity for members of the family to come together with the professionals and contribute to the process of shared decision-making. Table 8.2 again discusses the general EPP action steps that may be considered with all families, followed by a set of specific action steps that can be used with the Craig family in particular.

Discussion: The Participatory Phase (FGC) with the Craig Family

Once the preliminary phase is complete, the family and workers move on to the participatory phase, or the Family Group Conference. A number of the Craigs' extended family attended the meeting: Mrs. Craig's mother, sister, and brother-in-law, together with Mr. Craig's sister and her husband. Also at the meeting was a worker from a men's nonviolence program who had been introduced to the family during the preliminary phase, and a local child psychologist who had undertaken the in-care assessment of Billy.

An aspect of the professional role during the meeting is the generation of family confidence that the coordinator is able to manage the meeting process. Acknowledging the difficulties in working through children's issues in the midst of family tensions and problems can provide a basis for discussing the relationship between violence toward children and wider family violence. It is important that this discussion be made explicit

Table 8.2 EPP Participatory Phase: Case Study 1: The Craig Family

EPP Central Requirements	General EPP Action Steps (to be considered with all families)	Specific Considerations: The Craig Family		
		Development of Professional Skills	Development of family skills
1. Identifying skills and generating hope	1. Begin with appropriate cultural protocol 2. FGC process, aims, and goals discussed 3. EPP central requirements reiterated 4. Family problem-solving skills encouraged	* Generate family confidence in ability to manage meeting process * Respond to conflict as it arises * Acknowledge difficulty in working through children's issues when family problems create tensions and fears	* Create context within which family members can clarify and question * Identify positive aspects of family child care and family functioning
2. Blending professional and family skills	1. Full worker / case information shared 2. Family encouraged to question and clarify 3. Shared decision-making concept promoted 4. Facilitate agreement between worker and family to safety care plan	* Comprehensive provision of expert knowledge re violence issues; patterns of family violence etc. * Assess receptivity to accessing support services * Respond clearly and openly to questions when raised	* Encourage discussion by famliy 'experts' * Family consideration of access to the utilization of services (e.g. violence programs)
3. Managing issues of power in family	1. Encourage participation from all members	* Monitor contribution by family	* Exploration of individual and family response to

systems and family/worker systems	2. Enable views to be expressed by proxy if necessary 3. Explore range of ways in which views may be expressed 4. Avoid worker domination of process	* Be alert to domination of process by individuals in meeting * Be prepared to intervene if necessary (a) meeting process (b) the statutory minimum care standards for the children
4. Protecting vulnerable members	1. Facilitate implementation of safety support plan 2. Be cognizant of power dynamics during conference 3. Intervene if necessary 4. Ensure protection in planning and review phase	* Monitor contribution by family * Take 'time out' if necessary * Be prepared to put meeting into recess if intimidation occurs * Family responsibility for protection of members reinforced * Safety support plans actioned as required
5. Empowering and encouraging participatory practice	1. Ensure opportunity for private family deliberation 2. Encourage family problem-resolution skills 3. Ensure availability of information for family 4. Provide for family/client determined time frame 5. Attend to cultural protocols	* Draw on earlier preparation with family to contribute their views of decision-making process * Ensure family members comfort with and confidence in decision-making strategy * Family determined process by which decisions are made and negotiate with worker to establish agreed terms re decision-making

and that the family be clear about how family dynamics impact on decision-making processes. While not understating the difficulties faced by the family, the positive aspects of the family's child care and general family functioning, wherever possible, should be identified and discussed, for example, the fact that family members are concerned and caring enough to attend the meeting. It is upon these strengths that conference decisions can build.

In all Family Group Conferences it is essential that professional expert knowledge is fully shared. This is never more important, though, than in situations of domestic violence. The family need to know about patterns of family violence, and the impact this has on family functioning. Workers need to feel sufficiently confident to be able to respond openly to questions when raised, and to be clear about their position with respect to minimum standards of care for the children. Again, the worker needs to be able to discuss the violence in the family and to communicate the links between child abuse and wider family violence. It is useful to discuss treatment and support services, and the receptiveness of individuals to treatment should be assessed. At all times, the services should be cognizant of the violence within the family. In situations of domestic violence and child abuse, this can help to avoid the possibility of the problem being redefined and responsibility blurred.

Even though preparation for the FGC may have been thorough, the potential for intimidatory dynamics during the meeting cannot be underestimated. As previously mentioned, intimidation and messages of suppression can be subtle. A look or gesture from a violent perpetrator can be highly effective in controlling his victim's behavior. This is why gender-specific treatment is appropriate before moving into a family-solution-based child protection meeting. Even when the violent perpetrator is in treatment, it is important that during an FGC the worker carefully monitor the contributions made by family members, and that he or she remain generally alert to domination of process by an individual, and more specifically watch for any intimidatory behavior. Further, the worker needs to be able and prepared to intervene if such dynamics occur, and put the meeting into recess if necessary.

With respect to the family, opportunity should be provided for them to explore individual and group responses to the process of the meeting, and the issues raised at the meeting. In this book we have mentioned the benefits of private family deliberation during the FGC. While this is a principle that we strongly support in general, private deliberation, without any professional involvement, must be very carefully considered in situations of domestic violence. Individual safety must not be compromised for the sake of principles. Decisions about the position with regard to private family deliberation need to be made during the preliminary phase. The family, and individuals within the family, can be given the opportunity to determine the process by which decisions are made and that this must be one in which they have confidence. The protection of vulnerable members within the FGC is both a professional and family responsibility. Strategies for providing protection through the establishment of safety support plans are developed in the preliminary phase, and actioned during the meeting itself.

The purpose of participatory practice in the child protection area is to provide an opportunity for all family members to consider the issues, and to contribute to a process of decision-making with respect to the child. Within the Craig case scenario, domestic violence adds a layer of complexity that demands particular strategies, requiring an expert knowledge base and skills repertoire. Families going through the process of shared decision-making differ, and the knowledge and skills repertoire employed to assist them may also differ. In the next case study, we will consider the challenges faced by a migrant family, and will explore the complexities of developing a family-focused approach with an isolated family group.

CASE STUDY 2: THE MOHAMMAD FAMILY

The Mohammad family are Egyptian and have only recently, within the previous twelve months, migrated from their homeland. They have two children aged seven and five. The children came to the notice of protective services after a house fire revealed that the children were left alone at night. On further investigation, the youngest child was found to have a severe ear infection, causing deafness. The school reported that the older child had missed many weeks of school that year, and that the younger child was not enrolled and had not attended any school in the local area.

Mr. and Mrs. Mohammad both worked at night, Mr. Mohammad in a cleaning job and Mrs. Mohammad in a factory. They are a low-income family and both parents work long hours. They pay a high rent for substandard accommodation, and there is no money for health care either for themselves or the children. In addition to this, there are significant language difficulties, and the family have been subjected to low-level hostility from a particular group of young people in the community. Although the family have a large extended family network in Egypt, they have no relatives at all in their adopted land.

EPP Preliminary Phase: The Mohammad Family

Using the same approach as we used with the Craig family, we will now consider the particular action steps that are relevant to work with Mr. and Mrs. Mohammad during the preliminary phase. Table 8.3 once again explores the general EPP action steps that can be considered with all families, and considers the Mohammads' situation in particular.

Discussion: The Preliminary Phase with
the Mohammad Family

The cultural context surrounding this family provides the central organizing principle for understanding and undertaking the preliminary work with Mr. and Mrs. Mohammad. If there is a language difficulty, the first step is to engage an interpreter. Initial communication with the family clearly demonstrated the isolation they had faced since their move from Egypt. When it is established that extended family do not exist or are unavailable, as in this situation, one aim of the preliminary work is to begin building support and linking the family to wider community systems. However, in order to do this, the worker needs to better understand the processes of immigration, adaptation, integration, and minority marginalization faced by many immigrants. If the worker's cultural knowledge is underdeveloped, then the identification and engagement of cultural advice is essential. With regard to cultural advice it is wise to remember that although we sometimes think them so, countries within a geographical area are not necessarily homogeneous. Cultural boundaries are often strong, and may also be defined by religion. Here, the family needs to provide guidance, and so seeking their opinion and consent is important. With the appropriate cultural advisor, the worker can begin to develop a knowledge of the resources available, for example, within the cultural community, and add to his or her own knowledge of general services and entitlements that are accessible to families in need.

When a family such as this one comes to the notice of protective services, it can be a frightening experience for them, made all the more traumatic by language difficulties. State systems across different countries can be very different, and so the need for a full and clear explanation of the legal system and intervention mandate is essential, as is the monitoring of the family's understanding of this information. The parents may fear the loss of their children, and a lack of understanding about what is unfolding around them may increase their panic. Since the involvement of family in child protection decision-making is relatively new across child protection systems worldwide, there is a likelihood that the family will have all kinds of assumptions about things being taken out of their hands. Getting the point across about participation in these situations is therefore particularly important.

This reinforces the need for the worker to build an alliance with the cultural advisor. As with all working relationships, there needs to be discussion about and clarification of roles. Ultimately, the challenge for workers undertaking cross-cultural work in this area is to find a fit between cultural protocol and mandated intervention. Working with the culture rather than against it, while at the same time not forsaking child safety principles, is the aim of the work. Encouraging the family to talk about the ways in which child protection is managed in their country of origin and what the process of transition has been like for them coming to a new country can provide information that might help the worker assess the family's adjustment. Clarifying cultural norms with regard to parenting and child care and comparing these differences across cultural boundaries can have many benefits. First, it can tap into the family's own strengths. Second, it can make clearer to the family how expectations may differ from country to country with respect to child protection and the systems that work toward it. It can also help the worker and the cultural advisor to assess what community support is necessary to help the family. Linking Mr. and Mrs. Mohammad to other migrant families can help to build the family's supportive network. Talking about how families from different cultures manage their own internal difficulties, for example, deficits in child care and management, and how decisions are made around these family situations can also be helpful. Some cultural values and traditions may have a sympathetic fit with the concept of shared decision-making and collective responsibility for child welfare, and the FGC model may be compatible with many cultural situations.

Cultural values and traditions can also present challenges. Hierarchies within families and communities are often culturally determined and they may not rest easily with workers from another culture. What looks like outright sexism from one cultural perspective can have very different meanings in another. Cross-cultural processes of communication can be confusing. Respecting cultural traditions and learning to work with them rather than against them can help the family adjust to new and sometimes alien expectations. Again, finding a fit between cultural process and child protection procedure can do much to strengthen the work.

The purpose of the preliminary phase is to strengthen the decision-making process in the following stage. Children need to be protected during this time and there may be some urgent matters that require attention, for example, temporary care arrangements after school and in the evenings, and medical attention. The family needs to be aware of the

Table 8.3 EPP Preliminary Phase: Case Study 2: The Mohammad Family

	General EPP Action Steps (to be considered with all families)	Specific Considerations: The Mohammad Family	
EPP Central Requirements		Development of Professional Skills	Development of family skills

1. Identifying skills and generating hope	1. Preliminary meetings with parents
	  * assessment of necessary prelim work
	  * discussion of EPP central requirements
	  * comprehensive genealogy
	2. Cultural needs assessment
	  * consultants identified as required
	3. Preliminary meetings with family and/or support
	  * assessment of preliminary work required
	  * further develop genealogy
	  * discussion of EEP central requirements
	4. Submeetings as required
		* Understand processes of immigration, adaptation, integration and minority marginalization
		* Develop knowledge of Egyptian resources and cultural advice
		* Engage consultants
		* Use interpreter service as required
		* Clarify resource services and entitlements
			* Explore process of transition from previous lifestyle
			* Linking to other migrant families
			* Encourage storytelling of family support in country of origin

2. Blending professional and family skills	1. Preliminary meetings with workers
	  * discussion of EEP central requirements
	  * identification of possible philosophical/practice conflicts
	  * resolve worker conflict
		* Full explanation of legal systems and interventive mandate
		* Develop worker/client alliance
		* Engage support of school
		* Use cultural consultant to monitor family
			* Clarification of cultural norms re parenting and child care
			* Explore and compare differences across cultural boundaries

116

3. Managing issues of power in family systems and family/worker systems	2. Identify cultural supports 1. Submeetings of critical individuals, diads, etc., e.g., women, support team 2. Discussion of complexities of family and family/worker dynamics	understanding of process * Develop awareness of cultural hierarchies within family and community * Explore strategies for working with these * Broaden experience of community support, e.g., church if appropriate * Clarify roles and mandates of workers and cultural advisor and build working alliance	* Clarify how family views can be expressed * Clarify need and use of spokespersons if required
4. Protecting vulnerable members	1. Identification of safety issues 2. Establishment of support systems 3. Submeetings to establish safety support plan	* Ensure safety and care needs of children	* Identify temporary care arrangements for children after school and evenings * Work with professionals re health check for children
5. Empowering and encouraging participatory practice	1. Individuals prepared for FDM process 2. Family prepared for FDM process 3. Encourage thinking around need for services 4. Discourage premature adoption of professional strategies and plans	* Clarify decision-making process with family, rights and responsibilities * Ensure full comprehension of process, which may include information sheet in Egyptian	* Begin exploring strategies for community protection, i.e., community advocacy * Identify support persons throughout next phase

decision-making process to come and their rights and responsibilities in regard to this. Having this available to the family in written form (in their own language) can also be most helpful. Harnessing the cultural strengths of the family, and helping to build supportive networks are central to the strengthening of decision-making potential.

EPP Participatory Phase (FGC): The Mohammad Family

After successfully completing the preliminary phase, the Mohammad family and the professionals are ready to take part in the family group conference. Table 8.4 considers skill development within the participatory phase.

Discussion: The Participatory Phase (FGC) with the Mohammad Family

In some ways, if a comprehensive preliminary phase is undertaken, which includes the development of the family's support network, the clarification of the family's resource services and entitlements, and attending to the immediate care and safety concerns of the children, it calls into question the need for an FGC. Indeed, in New Zealand, use of the less formal family / *whanau* agreement[1] would be considered in these situations. However, with the Mohammad family, the emergency arrangements set in place during the preliminary phase could not be guaranteed in the long term, and there remained issues around the family's liaison with the school and their acceptance within the wider community. It was considered, therefore, that a family group conference was needed to consolidate the work done during the preliminary phase, and to establish future plans for the children's ongoing care.

At Mr. Mohammad's request, the sheikh from the local mosque attended the meeting. Although the family were of the Muslim faith, they had not had any involvement with the mosque since their move to the country. Another migrant couple also attended the meeting who were associated with the mosque and who had recently befriended Mr. and Mrs. Mohammad after their approach to the sheikh. The worker and the cultural advisor also attended. The conference was held at Mr. and Mrs. Mohammad's home, and the meeting began with a prayer.

Being flexible with the venue and being prepared to adjust to the family's wishes was important not only to Mr. and Mrs. Mohammad, but also to the other people at the meeting. The worker's sensitivity to cultural protocol, the use of time, and prayer, reinforced the family's commitment, ownership, and agency over process. In supporting a family strengths perspective and in particular the cultural strengths of this family, the worker felt able to speak honestly about the challenges confronting the family, and the need for a collective response toward finding enduring solutions. In this regard the tone of the meeting was solution-focused rather than problem-centered.

Building on the work done in the preliminary phase, the worker explored with the group some of the traditional strengths of the culture with regard to parenting and child rearing. The meeting then considered the minimum standards of care articulated by the worker, and the group moved into the private deliberation part of the meeting. In fact, the only person not present during this was the worker. All others present were considered part of the "family group" for the purposes of decision-making.

COMMENTS

These two case studies illustrate how the use of a family group conference can help to facilitate participatory practice with families in very different family situations. In both cases the nature of the difficulties provided a challenge to worker-family cooperation and partnership. However, by understanding the ecology of the family, and by developing a process that fits that ecology, a worker can mobilize strengths, and can facilitate processes that are relevant and meaningful to the families involved. If you are committed to a shared decision-making process, then you also need to find ways in which that process can harness the family's strengths. If a family does not understand the worker's child protection mandate and the commitment to participatory practice, then barriers to cooperation can emerge and can restrict the family's potential to do their best for their children. Maintaining a participatory approach throughout the stages of child protection work can be difficult when competing interests reinforce adversarial positions. However, establishing partnership and cooperation with family during the first two phases of the work can provide a sound basis for ongoing review and support. By using the central requirements of the Effective Participatory Practice model as a guide at the beginning and throughout all phases of the work, it is hoped that a pattern of participatory practice can emerge that develops both worker's and family's participatory skills.

Table 8.4 EPP Participatory Phase: Case Study 2: The Mohammad Family

EPP Central Requirements	General EPP Action Steps (to be considered with all families)	Specific Considerations: The Mohammad Family	
		Development of Professional Skills	Development of family skills
1. Identifying skills and generating hope	1. Begin with appropriate cultural protocol 2. FGC process, aims and goals discussed 3. EPP central requirements reiterated 4. Family problem-solution skills encouraged	* Be flexible with regard to venue e.g., the family home * Demonstrate preparedness to adjust to family's wishes * Emphasize solution-focused nature of process rather than problem-centered * Acknowledge difficulty in working through children's issues when families (and particularly parents) are under pressure	* Acknowledge family strengths)particularly cultural strengths) and capacity and willingness to work through issues * Encourage family responsibility and ownership of cultural aspects of process
2. Blending professional and family skills	1. Full worker/case information shared 2. Family encouraged to question and clarify 3. Shared decision-making concept promoted 4. Facilitate agreement between worker and family to saftey care plan	* Clarification of resources, both community and state * Sharing of professional expertise re child care and safety * Building of joint understanding with family with respect to this	* Establish with the worker agreed standards of care for the children * Clarification of resources within the families and communities * Sharing of family and support persons skills and knowledge of child care and parenting
3. Managing issues of power in family	1. Encourage participation from all members	* Explanation of professionals' role in	* Opportunity created for family to give response to:

systems and family/worker systems	2. Enable views to be expressed by proxy if necessary 3. Explore range of ways in which views may be expressed 4. Avoid worker domination of process	ongoing monitoring * Acknowledgment and clarification of powers invested in mandated role * Clear communication of acceptable levels and standards of care	(a) worker's mandated role (b) required standards of care
4. Protecting vulnerable members	1. Facilitate implementation of safety support plan 2. Be cognizant of power dynamics during conference 3. Intervene if necessary 4. Ensure protection in planning and review phase	* Workers have access to advisors throughout process * Safety and care needs of the child protected	* Family members provided with necessary support * Discussion of protective role of family facilitated
5. Empowering and encouraging participatory practice	1. Ensure opportunity for private family deliberation * Encourage family problem-resolution skills and potential re development of plan * Ensure availability of information for family * Provide for family/client determined time frame * Attend to cultural protocols	* Workers open to and respecting of cultural processes relating to decision-making and communication	* Family identification of decision-making process that offers cultural fit

NOTE

1. Family/*whanau* agreements are short-term agreements for services and general assistance to families and include such services as domiciliary help, parent education, respite care, and social work support. Family/*whanau* agreements seek to prevent the escalation of family difficulties, which can result in more intrusive statutory interventions, for example, the family group conference or court action.

9

Conclusions

Throughout this book we have argued a case for participatory practice with families in child protection. The worldwide trend toward this kind of family involvement is a movement that will bring many challenges to child welfare, in terms of both frontline practice and policy development. It seems that the question is no longer whether family should be an active partner in child protection processes, but how systems can be developed to enhance family involvement and demonstrate a commitment to empowering the family for the benefit of the child. Internationally these developments have occurred within statutory and nonstatutory frameworks, and have explored the possibilities of using cultural processes to enhance decision-making across a range of family situations. Partnership practice with families can be seen to have developed along a continuum from individual practice by committed individuals, to projects developed by agencies, to more radical changes in national policy and law. Common to these initiatives are the notion of the family as a system, the strengthening and maintenance of kinship bonds, cultural relevancy, and the use of community and state resources in support of families. These concepts resonate strongly with the values of social work, and as a profession social work in particular has much to contribute to the development of participatory practice. In closing we will briefly consider some of the wider issues with respect to using family group conferences within child protection, particularly the costs and benefits of using family decision-making forums. We will also explore the wider applicability of the shared decision-making process in other areas of family practice.

As countries develop their partnership initiatives, questions about the benefits and costs, both social and economic, will inevitably be asked. In New Zealand the family group conference is a statutory process that serves to divert families from the more formal and more expensive court process.[1] For the 1996–1997 year, 18,467 child protection notifications were accepted for investigation (New Zealand Department of Social Welfare 1997). During the same reporting period there were 3,688 family group conference outcomes, 88.8 percent of which reached agreement on decisions. The average cost of a family group conference has been calculated as NZ$1,603.[2] Family group conferences that reach agreement are unlikely to be referred to the court system, although in unusual cases the family group conference may agree that it is in the child's best interest that protections be sought through the court. The conferences that are unable to reach agreement are more likely to be referred to court for resolution: a much smaller percentage of conferences overall (11.2 percent). While it is difficult to say whether family group conferences do, indeed, save money, the fact that fewer families are being referred to court would suggest that savings are more likely with the new system. There may also be cost savings in the placement area when family placements are more enduring than out-of-home placements. However, if the family group conference system is to prove beneficial in the longer term, service providers will need to realize that good outcomes invariably result from careful preparation and planning, and that this kind of work is not inexpensive. As we have discussed in earlier chapters, the need for good, solid after-conference support and monitoring is also important, and can mean the difference between success and failure with respect to long-term outcomes.

When we talk about child abuse and partnership with family, we often think of the complex and severe cases that present difficulties regardless of what system is used. It is important to remember that families presenting to protective services cover a wide range of situations and the social benefits of reestablishing familial links and developing family support systems cannot be underestimated. Broadening the safety net for children by mobilizing extended family support also has the advantage that the responsibility for children's safety becomes a shared one between state and family. Working in partnership with families can also positively influence the adversarial relationships that can develop between worker and family in the child protection area. According to Marsh and Crow (1998) the benefits of using family group conferences include the healing of family rifts, indications of a lower reabuse rate and, more generally, the potential for services to have an improved public image. For the social worker, benefits can include the use of the process to move the case on when casework progress gets stuck, a better clarity of role and responsibility, and the development of partnership practice expertise (Marsh and Crow 1998:174).

In exploring the costs and benefits of using a family group conference model of practice, the question of research development within this area demands urgent attention. As discussed in Chapter 4, thus far research initiatives have been led by countries such as the United Kingdom, the United States, and Australia. Generally these studies have focused on the process of family group conferencing, the experiences and perceptions of those involved in the process, and the impact this has had on service delivery. There is a pressing need for longer-term studies that look at the qualitative and enduring nature of decisions that impact critically on the lives of the children and families involved. New Zealand has been in a good position to undertake such research but has been hampered by a lack of funds and the state's reluctance to put resources into outcome evaluation. This must be remedied if we are to better understand and respond to the ongoing needs of children and families within the system.

In this book we have discussed the use of the family participatory model, which includes the mobilization of extended family supports, within the child protection area. The model also has wider application. In New Zealand, the family decision-making process is used within the criminal justice area with young offenders. When young people offend against the law the FGC process is used to divert them from the court system. As with the child care and protection family group conference, family and extended family are entitled to attend. In addition, the victim of any committed crime is also an entitled member of the youth justice conference. While the process is similar to that used in the child protection area, it is different in that it focuses on the offenses committed by the young person and is used as a decision-making forum with respect to disposition. As a consequence, youth justice conferences are typically much shorter and there are many more of them, usually twice the number of care and protection conferences. Perhaps not surprisingly, the use of family group conferences to decide and resolve youth justice matters has been more successful with some situations than with others. According to Maxwell and Morris (1996), claims of both remarkable success and devastating failure have been made based on anecdotal evidence. In a review of the research on youth justice family group conferences in New Zealand they conclude:

> Although an examination of practice demonstrates, as might be expected, imperfections, it also demonstrates the potential of family group conferences to achieve these goals (of diversion, restorative justice and cultural appropriateness) to a greater extent than the more traditional process of court hearings. (ibid.:108)

Family group conferences have also been used to review children in alternative care placements. When placed in alternative care arrangements a child's situation is reviewed regularly. In the past this has generally involved professionals making plans and decisions. Sometimes this has involved the court system. Since the development of the FGC process, decision-making with regard to short- and long-term planning has been shared, once again, with the child's original family. If the child has been fostered and has developed a psychological attachment to the caregiver, the foster parents are also entitled to attend the meeting and, because of this bond with the child, are entitled to participate in the decision-making as a family member. Bringing the family together in the process of planning provides an opportunity for the child to reestablish links with the original family, and for the family and foster family to work together in the best interests of the child. Hence, the notion of shared responsibility for children is reinforced.

In many ways, the family group conference process, or variations of it, could be used in any area where issues of care and placement are indicated. In Chapter 4 we discussed an Australian initiative that used family group conferences when mothers are imprisoned, resulting in care issues for the child. Bringing together family to resolve care issues for elderly people is another related area in which family group conferences can sometimes be used to good effect. Although clearly different from child protection, work with the elderly is again an area in which the support and participation of family and extended family can have beneficial results.

In this book we have argued against the notion of the family group conference being the most critical and important feature of the shared decision-making model. While not undervaluing the FGC as a decision-making forum, we see it as one stage of a three-part process. It is surrounded by what we consider to be the critically important preliminary phase and, of equal importance, the review and follow-up phase. Undertaken comprehensively, this practice package has the potential to address some of the contradictory issues and complexities that have emerged in recent years as workers have developed partnership practice with families in child protection. The developments emanating from the family group conference initiative are wide-ranging and bring interesting and challenging practices to child welfare. They do not offer a panacea for resolving child abuse, nor do they have all the answers for all the families presenting to protective services. But they do offer a hopeful vision with respect to the development of empowering family practice in child protection, and, in harnessing the strengths of the family, extended family, and the wider community, they can do much to increase the safety net for children at risk.

NOTES

1.   As mentioned in Chapter 8, the Family / *whanau* agreements are less formal family resolution services. These are short-term agreements for services and general assistance to families and include such services as domiciliary help, parent education, respite care, and social work support. Family / *whanau* agreements seek to prevent the escalation of family difficulties that can result in more intrusive statutory interventions, for example, the family group conference or court action.

2.   Our information here is from the "Business Plan" (July 1997 to June 1998) of the New Zealand Children, Young Persons & Their Families Service. NZCYPS has the statutory mandate for child protective services in New Zealand. At the time of writing (April 1998), the exchange rate for the NZ dollar is U.S. $0.545.

References

ABA Center on Children and the Law (1996). *Family Group Conferences in Child Abuse and Neglect Cases: Learning from the Experience of New Zealand,* edited by M. Hardin, with E. Cole, J. Mickens, and R. Lancour. Washington: Author.

Adams, R. (1996). *Social Work and Empowerment.* London: MacMillan.

Angus, J. H. (1991). "The Act: One Year On." *Social Work Review* 3(4, February).

Armitage, A. (1995). *Comparing the Policy of Aboriginal Assimilation: Australia, Canada, and New Zealand.* Vancouver: UBC.

Ballara, A. (1998). *Iwi: The Dynamics of Maori Tribal Organisation from c. 1769 to c. 1945.* Wellington: Victoria University Press.

Ban, P. (1994). "Preliminary Findings on Family Decision Making Project in the Victorian Child Protection System." *Australian Social Work* 47(1):34–36.

Ban, P. (1996). "Implementing and Evaluating Family Group Conferences with Children and Families in Victoria Australia." In *Family Group Conferences: Perspectives on policy and practice,* edited by J. Hudson, A. Morris, G. Maxwell, and B. Galaway. Australia: Federation.

Barbour, A. (1991). "Family Group Conferences: Context and consequences." *Social Work Review* 3(4):16–21.

Barker, P. (1986). *Basic Family Therapy.* London: Collins.

Berelowitz, M. (1995). "Partnership: A Clinical Perspective." In *Legislating for Harmony; Partnership under the Children Act 1989,* edited by F. Kaganas, M. King, and C. Piper. London: Jessica Kingsley.

Boushel, M., and Farmer, E. (1996). "Working with Families Where Children Are at Risk: Control and Empowerment." In *Pathways to empowerment,* edited by P. Parsloe. Venture: Birmingham.

Bradley, J. (1994). "Iwi and the Maatua Whangai Programme." In *Social Work in Action,* edited by R. Munford and M. Nash. Palmerston North: Dunmore.

Bradley, J. (1995). "'Before You Tango with Our Whanau You Better Know What Makes Us Tick': An Indigenous Approach to Social Work." *Social Work Review* 7(1):27–29.

Chestang, L. (1978). "The Delivery of Child Welfare Services to Minority Group Children and Their Families." In *Child Welfare Strategy in the Coming Years,* edited by A. Kadushin, DHEW Publication No. (OHDS) 78 30158. Office of Human Development Washington,: DC Services.

Cheyne, C., O'Brien, M., and Belgrave, M. (1997). *Social Policy in Aotearoa New Zealand: A Critical Introduction.* Auckland: Oxford University Press.

Cockburn, G. (1994). "The Children, Young Persons and Their Families Act." In *Social Work in Action,* edited by R. Munford and M. Nash. Palmerston North: Dunmore.

Connolly, M. (1994). "An Act of Empowerment: The Children, Young Persons and Their Families Act (1989)." *British Journal of Social Work* 24:87–100.

Connolly, M. (in progress). "Preadolescent Sexual Offending and the Family Networks of Adult Male Sex Offenders." University of Canterbury, Christchurch.

Connolly, M., and Wolf, S. (1995). "Services for Juvenile Sex Offenders: Issues in Establishing Programs." *Australian Social Work* 48(3, September):3–10.

Corby, B., Millar, M., and Young, L. (1996). "Parental Participation in Child Protection Work: Rethinking the Rhetoric." *British Journal of Social Work* 26:475–92.

Courtney, M. E. (1994). "Factors Associated with the Reunification of Foster Children with Their Families." *Social Service Review* 68:81–108.

Cowger, C. (1997). "Assessing Client Strengths: Assessment for Client Empowerment." In *The Strengths Perspective in Social Work Practice,* 2nd ed., edited by Saleebey D. New York: Longman.

Croft, S., and Beresford P. (1994). "A Participatory Approach to Social Work." In *Practising Social Work,* edited by C. Hanvey and T. Philpot. London: Routledge.

Culbertson, P. (1997). *Counselling Issues and South Pacific Communities.* Accent: Auckland.

Curtis, C. (1991). *How People Change: Inside and Outside Therapy* New York: Plenum.

Davidson, J. (1983). "Maori Prehistory: The State of the Art." *Journal of the Polynesian Society* 92(3, September):291–307.

Diduck, A. (1995). "Partnership: Reflections on Some Canadian Experiences." In *Legislating for Harmony; Partnership under the Children Act 1989,* edited by F. Kaganas, M. King, and C. Piper. London: Jessica Kingsley.

Dominelli, L. (1997). *Sociology for Social Work.* London: Macmillan.

Dunlop, K. (1996). "Unique Aspects of Aboriginal Child Protection Cases." Presentation to the Law Society of Manitoba: Legal Studies Department, Winnipeg, Manitoba, March.

Durie, M. (1994). *Whaiora: Maori Health Development.* Auckland: Oxford University Press.

Fanshel D., Finch S., and Grundy, J. (1990). *Foster Children in a Life Course Perspective.* New York: Columbia University Press.

Fisher, R., and Karger, H. J. (1997). *Social Work and Community in a Private World.* New York: Longman.

Fleras, A., and Elliott, J. L. (1992). *The Nations Within: Aboriginal-State Relations in Canada, the United States and New Zealand.* Toronto: Oxford University Press.

Fox-Harding, L. (1996). *Family, State and Social Policy.* London: Macmillan.

Frank, J. D. (1973). *Persuasion and Healing*, 2nd ed. Baltimore: Johns Hopkins University Press.

Frank, J. D. (1974). "Psychotherapy: The Restoration of Morale." *American Journal of Psychiatry* 131:271–74.

Frank, J. D. (1982). "Therapeutic Components Shared by All Psychotherapies." Pp. 73–122 in *The Master Lecture Series. Vol. 1. Psychotherapy Research and Behaviour Change*, edited by J. H. Harvel and M. M. Parks. Washington, DC: American Psychological Association.

Fulcher, L. (in press). "Acknowledging Culture in Child and Youth Care Practice." *Social Work Education*, theme issue: *Residential Child Care*.

Fulcher, L. C. (1997). "Changing Care in a Changing World: The Old and New Worlds." *Social Work Review* 9 (1, 2):20–26.

Garbarino, J., Stott, F., and the Faculty of the Erikson Institute (1992). *What Children Can Tell Us: Eliciting, Interpreting and Evaluating Critical Information from Children*. San Francisco: Jossey-Bass.

Germain C. B. (1991). *Human Behaviour in the Social Environment: An Ecological View*. New York: Columbia University Press.

Germain, C. B., and Gitterman, A. (1980). *The Life Model of Social Work Practice*. New York: Columbia University Press.

Gil, E. (1996). *Systemic Treatment of Families Who Abuse*. San Francisco: Jossey-Bass.

Gilligan, R. (1997). "Beyond Permanence? The Importance of Resilience in Child Placement Practice and Planning." *Adoption & Fostering* 21(1):12–20.

Goldfried, M. R. (1991). "Transtheoretical Ingredients in Therapeutic Change." In *How People Change: Inside and Outside Therapy*, edited by R. C. Curtis. New York: Plenum.

Gomm, R. (1993). "Issues of Power in Health and Welfare." In *Health, Welfare and Practice*, edited by J. Walmsley, J. Reynolds, P. Shakespeare, and R. Woolfe. London: Sage.

Graber, L., Keys, T., and White, J. (1996). "Family Group Decision-Making in the United States: The Case of Oregon." In *Family Group Conferences: Perspectives on Policy and Practice*, edited by J. Hudson, A. Morris, G. Maxwell, and B. Galaway. Australia: Federation.

Hamill, H. (1996). *Family Group Conferences in Child Care Practice*, Social Work Monographs 151. Norwich: UEA.

Hassall, I. (1996). "Origin and Development of Family Group Conferences." In *Family Group Conferences: Perspectives on Policy and Practice*, edited by J. Hudson, A. Morris, G. Maxwell, and B. Galaway. Australia: Federation.

Hodges, V. G. (1991). "Providing Culturally Sensitive Intensive Family Preservation Services to Ethnic Minority Families." In *Intensive Family Preservation Services: An Instructional Sourcebook*, edited by E. M. Tracy. Cleveland: Mandel School of Applied Social Sciences, Case Western Reserve University.

Huber, M. (1994). "Mediation around the Medicine Wheel." In *Social Work Processes*, 5th ed., edited by B. Compton and B. Galaway. Belmont, CA: Wadsworth.

Immarigeon, R. (1996). "Family Group Conferences in Canada and the United

States: An Overview." In *Family Group Conferences: Perspectives on Policy and EL1 Practice*, edited by J. Hudson, A. Morris, G. Maxwell, and B. Galaway. Australia: Federation.

Kaganas, F. (1995). "Partnership under the Children Act 1989: An Overview." In *Legislating for Harmony; Partnership under the Children Act 1989*, edited by F. Kaganas, M. King, and C. Piper. London: Jessica Kingsley.

Kroll, B. (1995). "Working with Children." In *Legislating for Harmony: Partnership under the Children Act 1989*, edited by F. Kaganas, M. King, and C. Piper. London: Jessica Kingsley.

Lieberman, S. (1979). *Transgenerational Family Therapy.* London: Croom Helm.

Longclaws, L. (1995). "Devalued People: A Shift in Paradigm to Address Assessment and Treatment." *Manitoba Social Worker* 27(2, March):1–10.

Longclaws, L., Galaway B., and Barkwell L. (1996). "Piloting Family Group Conferences for Young Aboriginal Offenders in Winnipeg, Canada." In *Family Group Conferences: Perspectives on Policy and Practice*, edited by J. Hudson, A. Morris, G. Maxwell, and B. Galaway. Australia: Federation.

Longclaws, L., Rosebush, P., and Barkwell, L. (1994). "Report of the Waywayseecappo First Nation Domestic Violence Project." *Canadian Journal of Native Studies* 14(2):341–75.

Lupton, C., Barnard, S., and Swall-Yarrington, M. (1995). *Family Planning?: An Evaluation of the Family Group Conference Model.* Report No. 31, Social Services Research and Information Unit, Portsmouth University, Portsmouth.

Maluccio, A. N., Krieger, R., and Pine, B. A. (1991). "Preserving Families through Reunification." In *Intensive Family Preservation Services: An Instructional Sourcebook*, edited by E. M. Tracy. Cleveland: Mandel School of Applied Social Sciences, Case Western Reserve University.

Marsh, P., and Crow, G. (1998). *Family Group Conferences in Child Welfare.* Oxford: Blackwell Science.

Matahaere, D. (1995). "Maori, the 'Eternally Comprised Noun': Complicity, Contradictions and Postcolonial Identities in the Age Of Biculturalism." *Women's Studies Journal* 11(1/2):15–24.

Maxwell, G., and Morris, A. (1996). "Research on Family Group Conferences with Young Offenders in New Zealand." In *Family Group Conferences: Perspectives on Policy and Practice*, edited by J. Hudson, A. Morris, G. Maxwell, and B. Galaway. Australia: Federation.

McKenzie, M. (1995). "It Takes Two to Participate: Partnership Challenges in Family Group Conferences." Pp. 165–69 in *Partnerships That Work, Proceedings of the Asia-Pacific Social Services Conference*, edited by D. J. McDonald and L. R. Cleave. Christchurch: University of Canterbury.

Ministerial Advisory Committee on a Maori Perspective for the Department of Social Welfare (1986). *Puao-te-Ata-tu (Daybreak)* Wellington: Department of Social Welfare.

Morris, A., Maxwell, G., Hudson, J., and Galaway, B. (1996). "Concluding Thoughts." In *Family Group Conferences: Perspectives on Policy and Practice*, edited by J. Hudson, A. Morris, G. Maxwell, and B. Galaway. Australia: Federation.

Nelson, K., and Landsman, M. (1992). *Alternative Models of Family Preservation: Family-Based Services in Context.* Illinois: Charles C. Thomas.

New Zealand Department of Social Welfare (1997). *Statistics Report.* Wellington: Department of Social Welfare.

Orange, C. (1987). *The Treaty of Waitangi.* Wellington: Bridget Williams.

Parsloe, P. (1996). *Pathways to Empowerment.* Birmingham: Venture.

Parton, N. (1985). *The Politics of Child Abuse.* London: Macmillan.

Parton, N., Thorpe, D., and Wattam, C. (1997). *Child Protection: Risk and the Moral Order.* London: MacMillan.

Payne, M. (1997). *Modern Social Work Theory,* 2nd ed. London: Macmillan.

Pecora, P. J., Whittaker, J. K., and Maluccio, A. N. (1992). *The Child Welfare Challenge: Policy, Practice and Research.* Hawthorne, NY: Aldine de Gruyter.

Pennell, J., and Burford G. (1996). "Attending to Context: Family Group Decision-Making in Canada." In *Family Group Conferences: Perspectives on Policy and Practice,* edited by J. Hudson, A. Morris, G. Maxwell, and B. Galaway. Australia: Federation.

Pilalis, J., Mamea, T., and Opai, S. (1988). *Dangerous Situations: The Report of the Independent Inquiry Team Reporting on the Circumstances of the Death of a Child.* Department of Social Welfare: Wellington.

Prasad, R. (1975). *Success and Failure in Foster Care in Auckland, New Zealand.* Unpublished M.A. thesis, Victoria University, Wellington.

Rangihau, J. (1992). "Being Maori." In *Te Ao Hurihuri: Aspects of Maoritanga,* edited by M. King. Auckland: Reed.

Robertson, J. (1996). "Research on Family Group Conferences in Child Welfare in New Zealand." In *Family Group Conferences: Perspectives on Policy and Practice,* edited by J. Hudson, A. Morris, G. Maxwell, and B. Galaway. Australia: Federation.

Rosenzweig, S. (1936). "Some Implicit Common Factors in Diverse Methods in Psychotherapy." *American Journal of Orthopsychiatry* 6:412–15.

Roy, R., and Frankel, H. (1995). *How Good Is Family Therapy? A Reassessment.* Toronto: University of Toronto Press.

Sachdev, P. S. (1997) "Personality Development in Traditional Maori Society and the Impact of Modernisation." In *Counselling Issues and South Pacific Communities,* edited by P. Culbertson. Auckland: Accent.

Saleebey, D. (Ed.) (1997). *The Strengths Perspective in Social Work Practice,* 2nd ed. New York: Longman.

Salmond, A. (1983) "The Study of Traditional Maori Society: The State of the Art." *Journal of the Polynesian Society* 92(3, September):309–31.

Scheiber A. (1995). "Collaborative Decision Making in Child Protection Cases." *Social Worker* 63(4, Winter).

Schuerman, J. R., Rzepnicki, T. L., and Littell, J. H. (1994). *Putting Families First: An Experiment in Family Preservation.* Hawthorne, NY: Aldine de Gruyter.

Swift K., and Longclaws L. (1995). "Foster Care Programming: Themes, Policy Implications and Research Agenda." In *Child Welfare in Canada: Research and Policy Implications,* edited by J. Hudson and B. Galaway. Toronto: Thompson.

Taylor, N. (1997). "The Voice of Children in Family Law." *Children's Issues Seminar Series of Children's Issues Centre*. Dunedin: University of Otago.

Thoburn, J. (1995). "Social Work and Families: Lessons from Research." In *Legislating for Harmony: Partnership under the Children Act 1989*, edited by F. Kaganas, M. King, and C. Piper. London: Jessica Kingsley.

Thoburn, J., Lewis, A., and Shemmings, D. (1995). *Paternalism or Partnership? Family Involvement in the Child Protection Process*. London: Jessica Kingsley.

Trute, B. (1998). "Going Beyond Gender-Specific Treatments in Wife Battering: Pro-Feminist Couple and Family Therapy." *Aggression and Violent Behaviour* 3(1)1–15.

White, L., and Jacobs, E. (1992). "Liberating Our Children: Liberating Our Nations." Report of the Aboriginal Committee Community Panel, Family and Children's Services Legislation Review, British Columbia.

Whittaker, J. K., Kinney, J., Tracey, E. M., and Booth, C. (Eds.) (1990). *Reaching High Risk Families: Intensive Family Preservation in Human Services*. Hawthorne, NY: Aldine de Gruyter.

Author Index

Subject Index